BIBLICAL FOUNDATIONS FOR BELIEF AND ACTION

Books by Gurdon C. Oxtoby

Published by The Westminster Press

Biblical Foundations for Belief and Action
Prediction and Fulfillment in the Bible

BIBLICAL FOUNDATIONS FOR BELIEF AND ACTION

By

Gurdon C. Oxtoby

THE WESTMINSTER PRESS
PHILADELPHIA

LIBRARY OF CONGRESS CATALOG CARD No. 68–17149

PUBLISHED BY THE WESTMINSTER PRESS ®
PHILADELPHIA, PENNSYLVANIA

PRINTED IN THE UNITED STATES OF AMERICA

TO MY FAMILY AND MY NIECE, BARBARA

CONTENTS

I · *Introduction*

The Christian religion, like all religions, is founded on certain basic insights and beliefs. Any course of reasonable action presupposes particular understandings from which it springs. If the presuppositions are incorrect, it is reasonably certain that resulting conduct will be faulty. Hence, it is important to examine the foundations of belief and action.

Christians look to the Bible for the sources of their faith. The Bible is the charter of Protestant Christianity. Here is the great tradition of the past, the developing wisdom of other generations, corrected and completed in the revelation that comes through Jesus Christ our Lord. Through the centuries, the Old and New Testaments have been treasured by the church as the basis of Christian thinking.

Because modern discoveries and the development of scientific method have brought revolutionary changes in the way we view the world, the Bible is not always regarded as supremely authoritative in our generation as it was in previous generations. Instead of accepting uncritically what is written there, the modern mood is to examine what it says and to weigh its statements carefully in consideration of viewpoints that are currently held to be valid. Moreover, the scientific and critical methods that prevail in our day are now applied to the Bible itself. Biblical scholarship not only seeks to discover the origins of the books of Scripture but investigates the background that lies behind them, the sources from which they may have drawn, and the particular circumstances that brought them into being in their present form. We try to find out whether changes have been introduced into the books subsequent to their composition. We compare ideas and concepts in the various books with those found in other books. In such ways we have come to discern the development of Biblical theology and thereby to evaluate the several stages through which it has passed.

If we are to adopt the modern, scientific attitude toward the Scriptures, what does this mean with respect to the teachings of the Bible? Are they valid in the latter third of the twentieth century? What cautions, if any, must be exercised as we regard them? Are they, indeed, relevant to the thinking of our time?

Christian theology holds that the truths taught in the Bible are timeless. The pattern of history is not considered as altering the truths of Biblical faith. They are considered valid for every age and every generation. At the same time, we are to understand also that with the progression of human history, new situations and new problems arise, to which the Biblical understandings are to be applied. Society today is quite different from what it was in Old Testament times, and the church of today confronts situations quite at variance with situations faced by the church in the first century of the Christian era. How does the changeless gospel relate to an age of change? Is there such a thing as a changeless gospel at all?

It is clearly apparent that Old Testament teaching arose in a context quite different from that in which we live today. The Hebrew civilization that flourished in the first pre-Christian millennium existed in a setting very different from the one in which we now live. Theirs was the culture of the Middle East in the days when Egypt, Babylonia, Assyria, Persia, Greece, and Rome were the leading world powers. The religions of these nations, as well as the religion of the Canaanites among whom Israel lived, have long since vanished. Was the religion of the Hebrews different? Or did the time come when it also should have passed away, like the religions of their neighbors? Are we archaic in holding that while the faiths of their contemporaries were dispensable, the faith of Israel is still valid?

The teaching of the apostles, of the Evangelists of the New Testament, and of Paul and other New Testament writers was in the setting of the Roman Empire of the first Christian century. Although we have inherited much from Roman law and custom, there is still the question whether attitudes and judgments, customs and opinions, characteristic of the twentieth century should be molded by the thought of nineteen centuries ago. It is with inquiries like these in mind that we have undertaken to examine characteristic themes of Biblical teaching, to evaluate them in the light of present-day knowledge and attitudes, and to consider whether they are at all relevant to life in the age in which we live.

Since a book of the scope of this present work cannot pretend to examine all the teachings of the Bible, six significant themes have been selected and examined in the light of current knowledge. These themes are from both the Old and the New Testament, and represent some of the central and significant contributions that the Bible has to make to Christian thought. They will be considered exegetically and historically, and evaluated in the light of their appropriateness to our day. They range from the beginnings of all things, in creation, to the ultimate goal of human society in the Kingdom of God. They include an evaluation of the Old Testament law in relation to the freedom inherent in the Christian gospel. The true response of the creature to the Creator is brought under consideration, together with the prophetic critique of that response. Human sin and error are considered, together with the doctrine of Christ's atonement for sin. Finally, there is the theme of Christ himself and his relation to the church.

Certainly a reexamination of some of the great themes of Biblical teaching is in order in these days. Changing standards and attitudes are characteristic of our time. It is the hope of the author that enduring values may be discovered in the themes treated, not for the sake of holding to some tradition of the past, but because, in days of change, we need to take into account the old as well as the new, what has been as well as what may be, with the possibility that permanent worth may be found to lie in what has been handed down from previous ages.

It is with this purpose in mind that we turn our attention to a selection of the great themes of Biblical teaching.

II · *Creation and Providence*

Let us first examine the theme "Creation and Providence." It is appropriate to start with this, for this is where the Bible itself begins. Likewise, the opening words of the Apostles' Creed are: "I believe in God the Father Almighty, Maker of heaven and earth." This is the faith of the church. Scripture holds that all that exists does so as a result of divine will and purpose.

At the outset, we should define exactly the terms we are using. The word "create" is the English translation of the Hebrew *bārā'*, which means "to bring something into being." In itself, the word does not necessarily mean to create out of nothing. Neither does it require something out of which to create. In the first verses of Genesis it is used to designate bringing order out of chaos. In the Old Testament it is used exclusively of divine activity. Only God can create. When man brings something new into being, Hebrew uses the common verb *'āsāh*, translated into English by the word "make." Thus there is a theological distinction between the two words.

The Creator is therefore the one who brought into being all that exists — physical things that can be seen, heard, or touched, as well as psychological phenomena that cannot be seen but are just as real, and invisible forces, such as gravitation, radiation, and the like. Scripture holds that they exist as a result of purposeful will.

"Providence" is a word derived from the Latin verb *providere*, meaning "to foresee" or "to provide for." It is "provision" for something. It describes the relation of Creator to creation. The Deists of another generation held that God had created the world, but had gone away and left it, much as one might wind a clock, set it aside, and leave it to run down. Whether the universe would someday run down would remain to be seen. The Biblical doctrine of providence holds that God has not left his creation but, rather, is in it continuously, and that through it he works his will. In point of fact, some scientists believe that creation is taking place today. If Einstein's theory of relativity is true, matter and energy are related, convertible one into the other. Creation could therefore be a continuing process. If so, is God still the author of it, still the Creator? What would be the relation of this to providence?

The approach that we shall employ is, of course, the approach that should be made by any up-to-date space-age Christian. We cannot afford to hide our head in the sand, as the proverbial ostrich is said to do, closing our eyes to what is about us, in an attempt to hold on to faith only in the expression of some bygone generation. Faith must be contemporary. Our consideration must be in terms of what we think today. If it makes sense to us in these terms, it is relevant; if it does not, then we shall have to consider seriously what the alternative may be.

BIBLICAL STATEMENTS CONCERNING CREATION

What, then, is the Biblical teaching about creation? In the Eighty-ninth Psalm we read:

> The heavens are thine, the earth also is thine;
>> the world and all that is in it, thou hast founded them.
> The north and the south, thou hast created them;
>> Tabor and Hermon joyously praise thy name.
>>>> (Ps. 89:11-12.)

That is to say, because God has made these things, they are the exhibition of his glory. It is the same teaching that is explicit in the opening words of the Twenty-fourth Psalm:

> The earth is the LORD's and the fulness thereof,
>> the world and those who dwell therein.
>>>> (Ps. 24:1.)

The fullness of the earth is, of course, the things that fill it. The earth and all that is in it belongs to God because he has founded it.

The One Hundredth Psalm states:

> Know that the LORD is God!
> It is he that made us, and we are his.
> (Ps. 100:3.)

This is the rendering of the Revised Standard Version. The King James Version reads:

> It is he that hath made us, and not we ourselves.

Why is there this difference between the two renderings? The answer lies in two Hebrew words that are pronounced *w'lo anachnu*. *Anachnu* means " we," and *w'lo,* depending on how it is spelled, means either " and not " or " and to him." The KJV understands it to mean " and not we [ourselves]." The RSV prefers " and to him we [belong]." This preference arises from the fact that we are dealing with Hebrew poetry. Since one characteristic of such poetry is parallelism, we might expect the next line to afford a clue as to which is really intended. Fortunately, this is the case. The next line supports the RSV:

> It is he that made us, and we are his;
> we are his people, and the sheep of his pasture.
> (Ps. 100:3.)

Psalm 104 contains a lengthy description of how God brought the world into being:

> Thou didst set the earth on its foundations,
> so that it should never be shaken.
> Thou didst cover it with the deep as with a garment;
> the waters stood above the mountains.
> At thy rebuke they fled;
> at the sound of thy thunder they took to flight.
> The mountains rose, the valleys sank down
> to the place which thou didst appoint for them.
> Thou didst set a bound which they should not pass,
> so that they might not again cover the earth.
> (Ps. 104:5-9.)

The verses that follow state that God made the springs of water from which the beasts drink and beside which the birds nest, that he planted the cedars, caused grass to grow, and filled the sea with all kinds of creatures. The psalm ends with praise of the Lord for all his works.

Passages like these could be paralleled in Job, chs. 26 and 38. God as Creator is a consistent theme of Old Testament teaching.

BIBLICAL ATTITUDES TOWARD PROVIDENCE

So it is also with the parallel theme of God's providence. Jesus emphasized it. Matthew 10:29 records that Jesus asked:

Are not two sparrows sold for a penny? And not one of them will fall to the ground without your Father's will.

It is of interest that the parallel passage in Luke 12:6 reads:

Are not five sparrows sold for two pennies? And not one of them is forgotten before God.

Two sparrows for one penny; five sparrows for two pennies — in man's estimate the fifth sparrow has no value at all, but in God's sight none is forgotten.

Jesus continued, speaking of the lilies of the field, how they grow. They do not toil or spin, yet in God's providence, "even Solomon in all his glory was not arrayed like one of these" (Luke 12:27). It is God's care that robes them with splendor. Both the Old and the New Testament teach this consistently. Instances need not be multiplied, for the truth seems to be self-evident. It applies also to God's people. He cares for those whom he has chosen. He is concerned with those who are the objects of his choice, and he has set his heart upon them, not because they are more in number, but because he loves them and fulfills a covenant with respect to them (Deut. 7:6-9).

THREE APPROACHES TO THE DOCTRINE OF CREATION

With this background in mind, let us examine the Biblical teaching with respect to creation. The Bible as a whole has three approaches. One is that which is adopted in the first chapter of

Genesis, where seven days are indicated in which God made all things by his word. A second approach is found in the second chapter of Genesis, in which God created a man, then planted a garden in which he might live, filled it with living creatures, and then made Eve to be his wife. A third approach is reflected in certain passages in The Psalms, Isaiah, and Job, which share in the old idea that prevailed among all the Semitic peoples, that creation is the result of the victory of deity over the forces of chaos. This was represented in Babylonia and Assyria by the myth of creation, which was that the abyss, the chaos which existed first, was personified. The primeval water gods, Apsu or Tiamat, were overthrown respectively by Ea or Marduk, who then proceeded to create the world by splitting the defeated god of chaos in two, using one half to make the heavens above and the other to make the earth below. Creation is thus pictured as the result of a tremendous struggle, requiring every strength that deity could muster.

The Hebrews were acquainted with this point of view, which is of course mythological, by which we mean that it is symbolic rather than historical. It is reflected in several places in the Old Testament. Among the references to God's creative acts mentioned in the twenty-sixth chapter of Job occurs this statement:

> By his power he stilled the sea;
>   by his understanding he smote Rahab.
> By his wind the heavens were made fair;
>   his hand pierced the fleeing serpent.
>   (Job 26:12-13.)

Again, in the same book:

> God will not turn back his anger;
>   beneath him bowed the helpers of Rahab.
>   (Job 9:13.)

The poem in the fifty-first chapter of Isaiah contains this reference:

> Awake, awake, put on strength,
>   O arm of the LORD;

> awake, as in days of old,
>> the generations of long ago.
> Was it not thou that didst cut Rahab in pieces,
>> that didst pierce the dragon?
>>>> (Isa. 51:9.)

Among the references to God's creative acts in Ps. 89 is included:

> Thou didst crush Rahab like a carcass,
>> thou didst scatter thy enemies with thy mighty arm.
>>> (Ps. 89:10.)

Rahab is a proper name, with the meaning "storm" or "arrogancy," and denotes a mythological sea monster, seemingly connected with the Semitic myth of Tiamat, the destroyer of God's order in the universe. The Hebrews retained this myth as one description of creation, but God the Lord replaced Ea or Marduk as the Creator. They pictured God as victorious over chaos, because this was the way in which their neighbors did it. It is a third representation of creation.

Most modern books on astronomy include a diagram of the solar system, as we now understand it to be. The sun is shown in the center, and orbiting around it are represented the several planets with their moons. Mercury and Venus are closest to the sun, then the earth, and still farther out are the rest of the planets. The several orbits are represented as a series of concentric circles or ellipses. No one informed as to modern science would take serious exception to this as a true and proper representation. In which direction should we turn our telescope to see the circle that indicates the orbit of the earth? Which way should we look to find the other concentric circles or ellipses? The answer, of course, is that it would be useless to search for them with telescope or camera, since there is really nothing there except the planet itself. In point of fact, the artist has drawn a picture of something that is not there in order to indicate something about what is there. Yet no one would accuse him of deception. He is not trying to mislead anyone by visibly representing something that is invisible. We accept what he has done without question.

Let us consider another illustration, familiar to us all. On a bright summer day we look up at the sky and remark that it is deep blue. Our friends agree with us. In the evening, as the sun sinks below the horizon, we comment that the sky is deep yellow, or orange, or bright red, or fading pink. Others would agree. Later, when darkness has fallen, and the night is moonless, we note that the sky is black, and in it shine the distant stars. In this day of orbiting man-made satellites, how high would we have to send one before it hit the area that is blue or red or black? Of course the answer is that we would never hit it, for there is nothing there. Is it credible in this scientific age that we could say that something which is not there is blue or red or black? Yet this is exactly what we do. Moreover, we teach our children that the sky is blue. We do not feel that we are misleading them, for when the time comes, they will be able to understand why this appears to be so. We know that the apparent blue color results from the refraction of light on dust particles in the atmosphere. We know that the colored sky at sunset is the result of further refraction by water vapor in the air. What we are doing is describing the world as we see it.

Again, we know that the earth is a sphere, and can prove it. But when we take our children to the beach and point out the ocean reaching to the far horizon, our description is of a level sea. So it was with the ancient Hebrews. Their description of the world in which they lived was the description of what they observed. Their science was not ours, but their modes of representation correspond to what they saw.

The Old Testament Idea of the World

We can readily appreciate the elements that comprised the Old Testament world. When the writers of the Old Testament described it, they saw an apparently flat earth. They knew that the land in which they lived was surrounded by oceans, if one went far enough. Overhead was the dome of the sky, and in it the sun, moon, and stars. They knew that when it rained, water came down from the sky. They knew that if a man dug into the earth, in most cases he eventually came to water, so there must be water under the earth, and water behind the sky. The Hebrews, therefore, thought of their world as something such as is shown in the diagram on the next page. In it, the earth is central, and over it is the dome of heaven, which they called *rāqia'*, a word that we translate as " firmament." The Hebrew word is from a root that means to " beat out " or to " beat thin," and thus they conceived it as a surface. On the surface were the sun, moon, and stars. Across it flew the birds. Above it they imagined a tremendous watery abyss, and below the land a continuation of this same abyss. Also, beneath the earth they conceived an underworld which they called Sheol, a land of shades where the sun did not shine, and to which all men went after death to continue a shadowy existence. It does not correspond to the later conception of hell, for it was not a place of punishment, and existence there was certain for everyone, and it was not to be desired. It was the inevitable final abode of men.

This representation is a fair description of the world as it appears. If we could ask the ancient Hebrews what the world is like, they would say that it is a flat earth, above which is the dome of the sky, or firmament, or heaven, where are located the sun, moon, and stars, by which we tell time. If they sought to describe the creation of this world, these are the elements that would enter into the description.

CREATION IN THE FIRST CHAPTER OF GENESIS

Similarly, the author of the first chapter of Genesis describes the beginning of the world.

> When God began to create the heavens and the earth, the earth was without form and void, and darkness was upon the face of the deep; and the Spirit of God was moving over the face of the waters. (Gen. 1:1-2.)

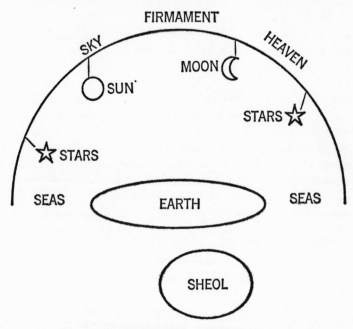

THE WATERS THAT ARE UNDER THE EARTH

THE ABYSS

Here is the representation of primeval chaos, the abyss of water of the Babylonian myth, whose name in Hebrew, *tehom,* is etymologically the same as the Babylonian *Tiamat*. Moreover, darkness was to the Hebrews not simply absence of light but an entity in itself. Isaiah 45:7 says of the Lord:

> I form light and create darkness,
> I make weal and create woe,
> I am the LORD, who do all these things.

Genesis continues:

> And God said, " Let there be light "; and there was light.
> And God saw that the light was good; and God separated
> the light from the darkness. God called the light Day, and
> the darkness he called Night. And there was evening and
> there was morning, one day.

> And God said, " Let there be a firmament in the midst of the
> waters, and let it separate the waters from the waters." And
> God made the firmament and separated the waters which
> were under the firmament from the waters which were above
> the firmament. And it was so. (Gen. 1:3-7.)

Reference to the diagram will show that the surface in the midst
of the waters is conceived as separating the watery abyss into two
parts.

> And God said, " Let the waters under the heavens be gathered
> together into one place, and let the dry land appear." And it
> was so. (Gen. 1:9.)

The space below the dome is cleared of water, and as it is
gathered to the sides, the dry land is understood to have appeared in the center, as shown in the diagram. The dry land is
named Earth, and the gathered waters are called Seas.

> And God said, " Let the earth put forth vegetation, plants
> yielding seed, and fruit trees bearing fruit in which is their
> seed, each according to its kind, upon the earth." And it
> was so. (Gen. 1:11.)

The earth is now considered to be covered with vegetation. Thus
the third day is brought to its conclusion.

On the fourth day God created the two great luminaries, the
sun and moon, and the stars also. They were set in their places
in the sky for signs and seasons, and for days and years, and to
give light on the earth. The fifth day saw the creation of fish to
swim in the sea, and of birds to soar in the firmament of heaven.

Finally, on the sixth day, were created animals of all kinds, and man himself.

> Then God said, " Let us make man in our image, after our likeness." (Gen. 1:26.)

This he did, creating man as male and female, and to him God gave dominion over all the works of his hand. They were destined to be fruitful and fill the earth and subdue it. Thus ended the sixth day. Then we read that on the seventh day God rested from all the works which he had made, and thus hallowed it.

The account is simple and dignified throughout. The trouble is that it raises questions that are disturbing to the modern mind. How could there be light before there were bodies that radiate light? If plants were made on the third day, and the sun was not created until the fourth, how could they grow? Plant growth is dependent on photosynthesis. Chlorophyll is essential, and it in turn is dependent on sunlight. If the sun had not yet come into being, how could there be plants of all kinds?

PROBLEMS RAISED BY MODERN SCIENCE

Thus the modern mind is perplexed by the first chapter of Genesis. It does not correspond to our understanding of the sequence of the created order. Only in general is there a resemblance to what is held by adherents of the evolutionary theory. How, then, shall it be regarded? Is it to be rejected as mythology? Or does it demand that the modern Christian abandon his scientific training, and adhere to something held long ago, simply in order to remain true to the faith? Finally, did all things come into being in the course of seven days of twenty-four hours each?

Here let it be said that the word " day " in Hebrew has the same latitude of meaning that it has in English. " Day " can be thought of in terms of " day and night," in which case day is twelve hours in length. Or we may speak of seven days a week, or thirty days a month, in which case " day " means twenty-four hours. But we may also speak of the " day " of George Washington, or of Abraham Lincoln, which means that we are thinking of the major part of a person's lifetime. If mention is made of the day of the Caesars, this would be something longer than a human lifetime, actually several lifetimes, or several centuries. The psalmist says that "a thousand years in thy sight are but as yesterday when it is past, or as a watch in the night" (Ps. 90:4). The Day of the Lord, referred to by many of the Old Testament prophets, is of indefinite duration. So, although the writer of Genesis speaks of "evening and morning, one day," the possibility of creation over a long stretch of time may not be excluded.

CATEGORIES OF CREATION

But what shall we say of the sequence that is here presented? Is this believable, or, indeed, rational? Is this the order in which things came into being? The following table sets forth what is ascribed to God's creative act on the several days in the first chapter of Genesis.

Genesis, Chapter One

Day	Creative act	Day	Creative act
1	Light	4	The luminaries that make light
2	Firmament, Sky, Heaven	5	Birds that fly in the firmament; fish that swim in the sea
3	Seas and dry land, Vegetation	6	Land animals, Man
		7	Sabbath of rest

What is here presented is not really an order in which created objects appear. What is set forth is in reality three categories of things that God has made, and the categories are twice repeated. On the first and fourth days, God made the light and the luminaries that cause the light. On the second and fifth days, God made the sky and the birds that fly before it. On the third and sixth days, God made what grows on the earth, and the animals and man who inhabit it. The author of Genesis is saying that God made three kinds of things: the light that illumines all creation;

the sky above and the earth beneath; and the things that surround us most immediately — plants, animals, and ourselves. The
writer looks to the things that are out yonder, far distant from
our human existence, then to the things that surround us more
closely, and finally, to the things that are our most immediate
concern. These are the three kinds of things which God has
made. Here is not an order of events, but a threefold classification,
twice repeated. The " days " are simply containers, as it were, for
the categories of created objects described.

When the first chapter of Genesis is regarded thus, it is seen as
one of the noblest of human descriptions of the origin of all that
is. Instead of finding here a conflict between ancient understandings and modern science, we have a most lucid statement
of the beginnings of the things we know. God is represented as
bringing all things into being by his " word." When God spoke,
his word was truth. When he said, " It is light," it was light.
When he said, " There is a firmament," it was so. When he said,
" Let us make man in our image," this was a description of what
had come to pass. The word of God was his deed. His statement
was accomplished fact. As he spoke, it was done. As can be demonstrated, this may have taken untold millions of years of time.
We are not dealing here with time sequences, but rather with
causal realities.

THE MAN IN THE GARDEN

There is also a second account of creation, found in the second
chapter of Genesis. This is the story of man in the garden. It
begins:

> In the day that the LORD God made the earth and the heavens,
> when no plant of the field was yet in the earth and no herb
> of the field had yet sprung up — for the LORD God had not
> caused it to rain upon the earth, and there was no man to till
> the ground; but a mist went up from the earth and watered
> the whole face of the ground — then the LORD God formed
> man of dust from the ground, and breathed into his nostrils

the breath of life; and man became a living being. And the
LORD God planted a garden in Eden, in the east; and there
he put the man whom he had formed. And out of the
ground the LORD God made to grow every tree that is pleasant
to the sight and good for food, the tree of life also in the
midst of the garden, and the tree of the knowledge of good
and evil. (Gen. 2:4-9.)

The word for " man " in Hebrew is *'ādām*. Here is Adam, made
out of dust from the ground, breathed into by the spirit of God.
The same word is used for " breath " as for " spirit " in Hebrew,
as is the case also in the Greek of the New Testament. Then, in
order that Adam might have a place to live, God created a garden
in the east, in Eden. The word " Eden " probably represents the
Babylonian *e-din-nu,* their designation of the Mesopotamian
plain. It is properly not a " garden of Eden," but a garden in
Eden, in the east. The designation of the location is indefinite. A
river is described as watering the garden, and dividing into four
branches, which are the four great rivers of the then known
ancient world — the Tigris, the Euphrates, and probably the
Indus and the Nile. The man is pictured as undertaking to water
and keep the garden.

The only instruction given by the Lord to Adam was:

You may freely eat of every tree of the garden; but of the
tree of the knowledge of good and evil you shall not eat, for
in the day that you eat of it you shall die. (Gen. 2:16-17.)

Then the Lord said:

It is not good that the man should be alone. I will make him
a helper fit for him. (Gen. 2:18.)

Adam fell into a deep sleep, and the Lord took part of his side,
formed a wife for him, and brought her to him. It is explained
that man said:

She shall be called Woman,
because she was taken out of Man.
(Gen. 2:23.)

The apparent wordplay in English is a true rendering of the word-play in Hebrew, in which the word for " man " is *ish* and the word for " woman " is *ishshāh*.

Then, of course, what does the man want to do? More than anything else he wants to eat of the fruit of the tree that was forbidden. He and his wife are pictured as being tempted by the serpent, as yielding to the temptation and eating the fruit. The result is that God thrusts them from the garden, and now the man must earn his living by the sweat of his brow. Here begin the woes of humankind. We refer to this as the sin of Adam.

What do we mean today by the sin of Adam? Is it credible that we are under some kind of condemnation as a result of something that Adam did long years ago? To ask this is to ask the wrong question. The word *'ādām* in Hebrew means " humanity." Adam is *the human race*. " Eve " means " living " or " life." Whom does God put into the garden? Humankind, with life to keep it perpetuated. What kind of garden? One which has everything in it that a person could ask. What does man do with it? He spoils the garden in which he has been placed. By self-will and disobedience he loses his wondrous heritage. The wrong question to ask is: Did Adam fall, and therefore we are punished? The real question is: Why is Adam fallen? You and I are Adam, and our whole generation is Adam. Why have we made a shambles of the garden in which we have been placed? These are the theological implications of this parable — for this story is not history in a real sense; rather, it is a parable of the human race in the world in which we are. With every opportunity to honor the Creator who put us here, we listen to the snake in the grass that says, " Go ahead! You will not die! " In point of fact, that is exactly what is wrong with the human race. Adam *is* fallen. His fall is on account of his own self-will.

This is one of the great themes of Biblical teaching: that man is fallen and in need of reconciliation. This is the human predicament. This is where the Bible is still relevant. Once again we remind ourselves that the Bible presents three concepts of creation: first, that God brings all into being by his divine purpose and will; second, that we see ourselves in the man in the garden who loses his inheritance; and third, in the representation that God slays the monsters of chaos and brings order into all things. This is the Biblical teaching concerning creation.

THE REGULARITY OF NATURE

We turn now to a consideration of the theme of providence. Providence indicates that God continues to provide for the world which he has brought into being. He has built into it seedtime and harvest, seasons, powers of reproduction and growth. He has put intelligence in man, and through the generations has revealed himself in nature, in history, through the words of prophets and teachers, and chiefly through his Son, Jesus Christ our Lord. In these ways he has given man guidance as to how to live. This is part of providence.

The modern mind tends to think of these provisions for the continuation of creation in terms of natural law. By this we mean that there is a regularity in nature, so that things may be expected to follow certain patterns. Natural laws are really descriptions of the way things usually operate. They are not legislation, so to speak, that cannot be suspended or violated. They are, instead, expectations as to what is normally to be anticipated. Yet there is a tendency of the modern mind to elevate natural law to a point where it may be supposed that matters cannot operate in any other way.

The law of gravitation, for example, indicates that if an object held in the hand is released, it will fall to the ground. Normally this is true. But a feather released in a breeze will not fall; it will float away. An iron nail released below a magnet will not fall, but fly upward toward the magnet. We explain these deviations from the basic principle in terms of other laws — of aerodynamics or magnetism — that counteract the law of gravity.

Likewise, there is a law of inertia, which holds that any object at rest will remain so unless something moves it, or any object in motion will continue to move in a straight line indefinitely unless something turns or stops it. Thus, a stone placed on the ground will remain there to eternity unless something moves it.

The planets circling the sun will continue to do so to eternity unless something interferes with their motion. Perhaps gravitation is
doing just that, for some scientists hold that the solar system is
gradually slowing down. The law of inertia may be thought of
as unvarying.

But consider this situation. On a hot summer day a dog is seen
lying motionless in the middle of the road. It is indeed a lazy
day. Suddenly the dog gets up and trots away. It is perfectly
obvious that nothing outside moved it. According to the law of
inertia, it should never have moved. Is this a violation of natural
law? Of course not. The dog is alive, and there are laws of
physiology that cut across the laws of mechanics so as to bring
about other results. Laws of life may counteract laws of physics.

But what about the laws of physiology? Do they inevitably
operate with complete regularity? Not at all. Let us assume that
I start from home in the morning, bound for the office, feeling
fine and fit, a spring in my step. I meet a friend who greets me,
saying: " Is something wrong with you today? Are you not feeling well? You don't look your usual self." I reply that I feel
fine, that there is nothing the matter with me. But in the next
block another acquaintance stops to ask if I am tired or was up
late the night before. He asserts that I have dark circles beneath
my eyes. I assure him that all is well, but now I begin to wonder.
By the time half a dozen persons have commented that I do not
look well, I arrive at the office, and find that I do have an incipient
headache. Presently I go home, really feeling poorly. I take my
temperature, and since it is above normal, I call the doctor. He
arrives, but his examination shows that there is nothing physically
wrong with me. My apparent affliction is purely psychological.
Thinking I am ill makes me so. Has some natural law of health
been violated? Not at all. Now we must note that there are laws
of the mind which cut across the laws of physiology, which, as
we have seen, cut across the laws of mechanics.

ARE MIRACLES POSSIBLE?

We have evidence, then, that there are, so to speak, layers of
natural law which interact, producing a variety of results. Things

do not always follow the expected pattern. How many layers of such law are there? We have noted three, but are there only three? Could there be four, or five, or several more? We have not yet completely unraveled the mysteries of God's providential ways. Could there indeed be a place in those ways for miracles? We must be careful not to equate a miracle with a violation of natural law, as is so often done. Miracles are not things that cannot happen. They are things that do happen. The sensitive person is surrounded every day by the miracles of God's providence. When we consider natural law, we must include the Biblical concept of miracle.

The word "miracle" is used infrequently in the English Bible. The RSV employs it in six instances in the Old Testament, always referring to wonders wrought in connection with the deliverance of the Hebrews from Pharaoh in the time of Moses. The plagues brought upon the Egyptians are termed miracles.

The word is used seven times in the New Testament. Simon the magician is said to have been amazed at miracles performed by Philip and those who were with him (Acts 8:13). It is said that "God did extraordinary miracles by the hands of Paul" (Acts 19:11). In the First Letter to the Corinthians, Paul speaks of the varieties of gifts given to members of the church:

> To one is given through the Spirit the utterance of wisdom, and to another the utterance of knowledge according to the same Spirit, to another faith by the same Spirit, to another gifts of healing by the one Spirit, to another the working of miracles, to another prophecy, to another the ability to distinguish between spirits, to another various kinds of tongues, to another the interpretation of tongues. (I Cor. 12:8-10.)

In this instance, what would members of the church do who are workers of miracles?

Actually, to use this term is sometimes misleading, because it is ambiguous. There are three Hebrew words and three Greek words whose use will help us appreciate what is involved in the idea of miracle. In Hebrew the words are 'oth, mophēth, and niphlāh.

'Oth in the Old Testament is properly translated "sign."

Moses does " signs " before Pharaoh. What is meant by " sign "? On any highway, a sign calls attention to something. That something may be a change of speed limit, the turnoff to a particular town, a reason for caution, or the distances to different cities. So also in Scripture a sign calls attention to something. It signifies something. It is therefore significant. Some of the things we call miracles are signposts pointing to particular truths or facts. As we have seen, according to the first chapter of Genesis, the sun, moon, and stars are said to be set in the sky " for signs and for seasons and for days and years " (Gen. 1:14). When Joshua led the Israelites across the Jordan, it is related that he set up a memorial of twelve stones, one for each tribe, the reason being

> that this may be a sign among you, when your children ask in time to come, " What do those stones mean to you? " Then you shall tell them that the waters of the Jordan were cut off before the ark of the covenant of the LORD. (Josh. 4:6-7.)

The word *mophēth* means a " portent," something that is striking or startling, as, for example, a catastrophe — an earthquake, a falling star, the eruption of a volcano. This kind of thing, which is outside the usual order of events, is a reminder of other values. By arresting attention, it compels us to reconsider facts and attitudes. Often, in the prophets, portents are connected with the end of the age and are pictured as the darkening of the sun, the turning of the moon into blood, and the occurrence of earthquakes in various places. These are reminders of God's judgment. Portents, therefore, are events that stir us from our complacency.

The third word, *niphlāh,* is from a root meaning " to wonder." Properly it is something " wonderful," or " producing wonder." Manifold in this world are things that produce wonder in the beholder. The writers of the Old Testament were aware of this. They shared in the wonder produced by the marvels of God's providence. So also should we.

In the New Testament, the acts of Jesus commonly referred to as miracles are not usually called such in the English translation. Three Greek words are used to express them. The first is *sēmeion,* which means a " sign " in exactly the same sense in which that word is used in the Old Testament. The sign called attention to something that lay behind it. It was the signification of a truth that might have been overlooked. The "signs" that Jesus did were pointers to the Kingdom of God, or pointers to God who is the Creator and whom Jesus called the Father who is in heaven.

A second word is *teras,* a "wonder," producing wonder in the beholder. Sometimes the wonder causes fear or consternation in the mind of him who observes it. It may be something that startles, much as "portent" does in the Old Testament. A person is alerted by a wonder to a reexamination of his point of view.

A third word, the one most frequently used of the miraculous deeds of Jesus, is *dynamis.* This is the word from which is derived our word "dynamic," as well as "dynamite" and other terms. It suggests power. Properly, in the New Testament it means "a mighty work" demonstrating power. The mighty works of Jesus are works of power. They convey a sense of authority. We read that the people were astonished at his teaching,

> for he taught them as one who had authority, and not as their scribes. (Matt. 7:29.)

What, then, is providence? It is the Creator's relation to his creation. It is God's relation to what he has made. It is God working through his servants, the prophets, and through his Son, Jesus Christ our Lord, to point the way toward his will for men. He is ready to provide for his people if his people will respond in a way that makes his provision possible.

He who created is characterized by works of providence. We tend to capitalize the word, and use it in a kind of impersonal way, as when we speak of trusting in Providence. Or, we may say, "Do not defy Providence by such a line of action." In such a connection, we are really substituting Providence for deity. What is really meant is, "Do not defy God," "Do not defy the Creator." There is no such thing as abstract providence that watches over us. There is no abstract providence that shapes our ends. Instead, there is a Creator, who, having brought us into being, is trying to lead us into the way by which we may truly come into our own, as sons of the Most High.

III · *Worship and Righteousness*

What should be the response of the creature to the Creator? How should he express his gratitude for having been brought into being? What responsibilities does he have because he is here? Should he do something to honor the God who made him, and if so, what? In what does God take delight, so far as the creature is concerned? This last is the age-old question in religion. As long as men have tried to do homage to deity, a great variety of forms and ceremonies have been devised to that end. The English word "worship" is derived from two elements, "worth" and the suffix "ship" denoting condition or profession. "Worship" is properly "worthship." It is the profession of the value or worth of the one being honored.

Let us illustrate this by a modern example. A person of real "worth" is to visit town. He may have distinguished himself in some remarkable way, he may have shown creative talents, or he may be a person who has made some great contribution to society. You are chairman of a committee to do him proper honor. What procedure do you suggest? Should there be a reception where members of the community can meet him? Should there be a banquet in his honor, with speeches? If so, who should make the speeches, the man himself or others who might tell about him? Would you have him entertained in private homes or in some public place? Should some event such as a concert be sponsored in his honor? Should there be contributions to some cause in which he may be interested? No doubt the choice among these depends in some considerable measure upon what kind of person he is. What is appropriate for one may not be so for another.

This is exactly the problem in the worship of God. According to the way in which men have regarded deity, they have worked out their worship response. All kinds of acts and ceremonies have been tried. Should there be a procession in honor of deity? Should there be music, and if so, of what kind? Should there be dancing or other similar ceremonies? Does one honor deity by feasting? or by fasting? Does eating certain foods or not eating certain foods do him honor? Is there some way in which one should dress or not dress? There are sects in Pennsylvania, Ohio, and elsewhere that, for religious reasons, will not use buttons on their clothes, or ride in automatically powered vehicles, for the honor of God. The ancient Egyptians believed that if they slaughtered their enemies before their gods, it would demonstrate their loyalty. The Canaanites, who believed in fertility gods, participated in sexual orgies, since they supposed this would honor them. And, of course, gifts to deity were well-nigh universal. How should they be sent to deity? Sacrifice is a very widespread phenomenon. What was burned went up to God as a gift. It could be incense, " an odor pleasing to the Lord," or it could be animals of the herd or flock, or produce of the fields.

The question of the worship of the Creator, one of the themes of Biblical teaching, has received a great deal of attention through the years. Let us examine what the Bible has to say, and see what conclusions we can draw that will be germane to the present day.

Worship Depends on Conception of Deity

The psalmist indicates some Old Testament reactions to the worship of the heathen:

> Our God is in the heavens;
>   he does whatever he pleases.
> Their idols are silver and gold,
>   the work of men's hands.
> They have mouths, but do not speak;
>   eyes, but do not see.
> They have ears, but do not hear;
>   noses, but do not smell.
> They have hands, but do not feel;

> feet, but do not walk;
> and they do not make a sound in their throat.
> Those who make them are like them;
> so are all who trust in them.
>
> (Ps. 115:3-8.)

In a very real sense this is true. The way we conceive of deity partly makes us what we are. " Those who make them are like them." If deity is conceived of as distant, transcendent, and abstract, worship tends to be formal, liturgical, and traditional. If God cannot be approached in reality, only formal representations are possible. Much of the worship of the sun-god in ancient Egypt was of this category. The sun-god was considered distant, even though sunlight and its warmth permeate everyday life. Hence, much of the worship ascribed to him was extremely ritualistic. Yet, in some worship formulas, Egyptians of the age of Ikhnaton thought of the sun disk as in a sense monotheistic, and some of the prayers of that era present a warmth and a spontaneity that differ remarkably from expressions of the centuries preceding.

If deity is conceived of as approachable because of a personal relationship between Creator and creature, worship becomes quite otherwise. It is thought of as a much more intimate relationship between persons. It is not merely reverence due to an imperial and transcendent divinity. It is the recognition of a definite and personal concern on the part of deity for creature, and a personal responsibility of the creature toward the one who brought him into being and constantly sustains him. The reason why the Psalter seems to stand so close to Christian feeling is that in it, more than anywhere else in the Old Testament, human relationship with God assumes a wide range and a more intimate, free manner. In the New Testament it was the presence of Christ among his disciples, followed by a vivid consciousness of his continuing presence with them after he was removed from their bodily sight, that brought about their worship of him. And since they became conscious of the deity that he embodied, this wrought a change in the attitude that they had toward the

Father himself. God was not regarded now as a far-off being of a nature so distinct from man that he could be approached only as an Oriental came to some great king. What may be called a despotic or autocratic view of the divine relation to men came to be replaced by a domestic or friendly view. The result of this was that worship came to be more familiar and many-sided. No longer was it merely distant reverence or servile recognition. It came to involve affection, loyalty, aspiration, and a confidence that were not previously possible.

The Christian practice of public worship, therefore, when developed to its conclusions, should be substantially much superior to its antecedents. It borrows heavily from what other peoples in other times have done, especially the Old Testament tradition. But Christian devotion, though it has adopted and assimilated much of what has gone before, takes on a new color and a new energy because of what we have learned from Christ about the Father who is in heaven. Christian prayers and hymns, for example, tended from the very first to contain a broader and a freer expression of human personality in close and confident relationship to the divine.

The Old Testament presents worship in several different aspects. There is a primitive stage, in which worship is very simple, consisting of giving sacrifice to God. It is displayed clearly in Genesis and also in The Book of Judges. There is very little organization; the head of the household offers sacrifice. Very few rules circumscribe the ceremony. It takes place wherever it seems appropriate. There seem to have been places where God was particularly available, as at the " oak of Moreh," the " oak of the teacher," or the " oak of the director " (Gen. 12:6; Deut. 11:30).

THE TABERNACLE

Exodus describes the Tabernacle in the wilderness. The traditional view is that this was derived from a divinely inspired revelation to Moses (Ex., chs. 25 to 30). An account is later given of the making and furnishing of the Tabernacle (Ex., chs. 35 to 40). Modern scholarship is of the opinion that this movable sanctuary as here described never really existed. It is an ideal structure, the product of priestly imagination. Its basis is probably in the Temple of Solomon, which it resembles not only in its general form, each dimension being one half the dimension of the Temple, but in details of furnishing and decoration. The later Temple is thus reflected back into the wilderness, and ascribed to Moses. This reflection includes the ideas of the one sanctuary, one altar, and one priestly family, which did not become current until the reformation of Josiah in 621 B.C.

The idea may be in part suggested by another tradition preserved in Exodus, that of the Tent of Meeting. This is not identified with the Tabernacle, and it is said to have been outside the camp, rather than in its midst, where the Tabernacle was pictured. The Tent of Meeting is represented as the place where Moses could meet with God. It was the place where the Lord " dwelt " and where Moses could meet him by appointment. " Meeting " is more properly " appointment." On this Tent the Lord descended in a cloud when Moses entered it, and there he spoke with him at the door of the Tent (Ex. 33:9).

From what has been said, it is evident that we do not know very much about Israelite worship during the wilderness wandering. When the Israelites settled in the Promised Land, the center of worship was evidently at Shiloh, at a shrine presided over by Eli and his sons. It must have been a very primitive structure, for Eli had a servant or two, and the boy Samuel was his helper. The Ark of the Covenant was kept here. It symbolized the presence of the Lord, and was furnished with rings through which staves could be passed so that the box could be carried in procession. The presence of the Lord was thus carried into battle against the Philistines, by whom it was captured, subsequently to be returned (I Sam., chs. 4 to 6). No elaborate ritual is indicated for the shrine at Shiloh. Worship was still evidently very simple and uncomplicated.

When Jerusalem was made the capital, and the country became prosperous in the days of Solomon, a royal complex was constructed on Mt. Zion. It was not so much a sacred hill as a royal hill. On its leveled summit was an enclosure in which Solomon erected a group of buildings intended for use by himself and his household. Some of these were designed for administrative purposes, but others were to be used simply as the residence of the king and his harem. The group included the royal palace and harem, the Porch of Pillars, the Throne Porch (Solomon's Porch), and the House of the Forest of Lebanon, the roof of which was supported by forty-five cedar pillars in three rows, giving rise to the name.

THE TEMPLE

Only after the palace complex was completed, a process that took thirteen years, did Solomon undertake the Temple, which may have been planned as a palace shrine, later assuming national significance. The Temple structure was in the form of a rectangle, 60 cubits in length, about 105 feet, if the " sacred cubit " of 21 inches is meant, 20 cubits in breadth, and 30 cubits in height. The interior was divided into two parts, the east entrance through the vestibule leading to the Holy Place, beyond which, in the form of a cube, was the Holy of Holies, or Most Holy Place, 20 cubits in each dimension. It had no windows, and if lighted at all, must have been artificially illuminated. In it was kept the Ark of the Covenant. It was separated from the Holy Place by a partition of cedar, in which were set two doors of cedar; and before it there seems to have been hung a veil.

The Holy Place, or sanctuary, was 40 cubits long, 20 wide, and 30 in height. Its walls were pierced by latticed windows, probably near the roof, for ventilation and the escape of smoke. The altar of incense was here, made of cedar overlaid with gold, as also were ten golden lampstands and ten tables, on one of which was placed the Bread of the Presence, sometimes called the shewbread.

The building was surrounded by storerooms, arranged in three stories, perhaps about thirty in number, though I Kings does not say how many there were. The building stood at the west end of a large enclosure, with the entrance facing east. In front of it, in the courtyard, was the altar of burnt offering and a bronze laver.

We should, of course, note that only the priests entered the building proper. Worshipers stood in the courtyard.

Recalling that the Temple was built by workmen furnished by Hiram, king of Tyre, it is not surprising that the decorations described in I Kings, ch. 7, conform closely to those recovered by archaeologists from Phoenician temples. The symbolism of palm trees, open flowers, and gourds, of oxen, lions, and cherubim, was the common symbolism of the Middle East. Moreover, in the ground plan, the courtyard, the vestibule, the Holy Place, and the inner Most Holy Place find their exact counterparts in Egyptian temples that stand today. The Hebrews shared the idea of what constituted a proper House of the Lord with their surrounding neighbors.

As we have said, a worshiper entering the Temple did not go into the building proper, but only into the courtyard. If we consider the call of Isaiah, as described in Isa., ch. 6, we read:

> In the year that King Uzziah died I saw the Lord sitting upon a throne, high and lifted up; and his train filled the temple. (Isa. 6:1.)

Isaiah was, of course, not in the building. Evidently he pictures himself as standing at one of the entrance gates, or possibly at the top of a flight of steps leading up to the courtyard. The Temple was yonder, across the court, and there, in what was known as the House of the Lord, he saw the Lord on his throne, with seraphim calling, "Holy, holy, holy is the LORD of hosts." In response to Isaiah's lament that he was a man of unclean lips in the midst of a people of unclean lips one of the seraphim flew to him, winging its way across the courtyard. At the altar of burnt offering he paused to take a hot coal with tongs, then continued to where Isaiah stood at the entrance. With the hot coal he purged the prophet's lips in symbolic action, and Isaiah, in response to the question, "Whom shall I send, and who will go for us?" answered, "Here am I! Send me." This is the kind of Temple arrangement we must have in mind.

In the eighth chapter of I Kings, the building of the Temple having been finished, the people are pictured gathered there for the dedication. Solomon is represented as offering a dedicatory prayer and benediction. It is a beautifully phrased liturgical composition. We are, of course, to understand that no stenographer was present to take down and preserve what he said. The books of Kings were written during the exile, or at least brought to their present form at that time, several hundred years later. This prayer was evidently composed by the author of the books of Kings and ascribed to Solomon. This was quite in line with what was done in ancient times. The Greek historians Herodotus and Thucydides, in describing battles in which the Greeks took part, put into the mouths of Greek generals, before they engaged in battle, beautifully composed orations, classic examples of Greek literature, wonderfully turned in thought and rhetoric. Everyone understands that these are the compositions of the historians, and that what was said on the field of battle was probably something quite different.

Solomon's prayer is an appeal to God to hearken when men pray in this place. Various situations are indicated where individuals, or the people as a whole, are in some kind of trouble. Then follows the refrain: " Yea, hear thou in heaven thy dwelling place; and when thou hearest, forgive." Although this is the Lord's house, he dwells in the highest heaven, coming to his people in response to their supplications. First Kings 8:34 includes the phrase, "Forgive the sin of thy people Israel, and bring them again to the land which thou gavest to their fathers." This implies their exile, a situation which Solomon could not have foreseen, and definitely indicates that the prayer was composed while the people longed for a return to their homeland.

Let us note especially the benediction at the end, when Solomon stood before the people and blessed the assembly with a loud voice, and said:

> Blessed be the LORD who has given rest to his people Israel, according to all that he promised; not one word has failed of all his good promise, which he uttered by Moses his servant. The LORD our God be with us, as he was with our fathers; may he not leave us or forsake us; that he may in-

cline our hearts to him, to walk in all his ways, and to keep
his commandments, his statutes, and his ordinances, which
he commanded our fathers. Let these words of mine, where-
with I have made supplication before the LORD, be near to
the LORD our God day and night, and may he maintain the
cause of his servant, and the cause of his people Israel, as each
day requires; that all the peoples of the earth may know that
the LORD is God; there is no other. (I Kings 8:56-60.)

The reference to "his commandments, his statutes, and his ordinances" shows the acquaintance of the author with Deuteronomy,
which was the basis of the reformation under Josiah, in 621 B.C.

We would do well to notice the three elements in this benediction: (1) "The LORD . . . be with us, as he was with our fathers."
Here is the recollection of history, and the prayer that the covenant relationship with God be continued. (2) "May he maintain
the cause . . . of his people . . . , as each day requires." Here
is the idea of one day at a time, not a series of days, or a line of
tomorrows, but today. It reminds us of the Lord's Prayer, "Give
us this day our daily bread" — properly, our bread for today,
not bread for tomorrow, but supplying our need for the present.
(3) "That all the peoples of the earth may know that the LORD
is God; there is no other." This is the universal element, the mis-
sionary thrust, which appears many times in the Old Testament.

WORSHIP IN THE TEMPLE

An examination of The Psalms will indicate the kind of worship
that was characteristic of the Temple. Psalm 92 reads:

> It is good to give thanks to the LORD,
>   to sing praises to thy name, O Most High;
> to declare thy steadfast love in the morning,
>   and thy faithfulness by night,
> to the music of the lute and the harp,
>   to the melody of the lyre.
> For thou, O LORD, hast made me glad by thy work;
>   at the works of thy hands I sing for joy.
>   (Ps. 92:1-4.)

This indicates that worship is joyous. It is not painfully solemn and lugubrious, but is undertaken with joy. Music and musical instruments are included.

The same is true of Ps. 100:

> Make a joyful noise to the LORD, all the lands!
>> Serve the LORD with gladness!
>> Come into his presence with singing!
>
> . . . .
>
> Enter his gates with thanksgiving,
>> and his courts with praise!
>> Give thanks to him, bless his name!
>
>> (Ps. 100:1-2, 4.)

Psalm 68 has the following description:

> Thy solemn processions are seen, O God,
>> the processions of my God, my King, into the sanctuary —
> the singers in front, the minstrels last,
>> between them maidens playing timbrels:
> " Bless God in the great congregation,
>> the LORD, O you who are of Israel's fountain! "
> There is Benjamin, the least of them, in the lead,
>> the princes of Judah in their throng,
>> the princes of Zebulun, the princes of Naphtali.
>
>> (Ps. 68:24-27.)

Psalm 24 mentions processions into the Temple. Psalm 81 reflects aspects of the forms of worship that prevailed:

> Sing aloud to God our strength;
>> shout for joy to the God of Jacob!
> Raise a song, sound the timbrel,
>> the sweet lyre with the harp.
> Blow the trumpet at the new moon,
>> at the full moon, on our feast day.
> For it is a statute for Israel,
>> an ordinance of the God of Jacob.
>
>> (Ps. 81:1-4.)

There are seasons for worship. Not only is the Sabbath held to be holy, but the new moon and the full moon as well. Probably the origins of this are very ancient, stemming from pagan customs of previous times, but on days of this kind it seemed appropriate to call attention to the great things the Lord has done.

After the return from the exile, the Temple was rebuilt. It was probably in considerable measure similar to the preexilic Temple. But the worship became more elaborate and probably drew upon additional ceremonies that the people had observed in Babylon. Worship in the Second Temple included splendid processions, priests in vestments, trumpets and musical instruments of various kinds, singing, dancing, and, of course, burnt offering and sacrifice of animals from the herds or flocks, or flour, bread, or cakes, as gifts to God. In the peace offering, the worshiper ate part of the food, and the rest was offered in sacrifice, so that the worshiper in effect sat at table with deity.

In our Christian custom, we have inherited much that belonged to worship in Old Testament times. With the dispersion of the Jews to various parts of the world, the time came when most of them could not attend worship in the Temple. Therefore, there arose the synagogue, its name being Greek and meaning " an assembling together." It is the equivalent of the Hebrew *qahal,* " congregation " or " assembly." It was the place where they came together to talk about the things of their faith. Since no priesthood was connected with it, there was no sacrifice, and other elements began to replace former customs. The psalms were read or sung; the Book of the Law was read, as were the Prophets; there would be comment on the Law; they would affirm their faith in the great words of Deuteronomy:

> Hear, O Israel: The LORD our God is one LORD; and you shall love the LORD your God with all your heart, and with all your soul, and with all your might. (Deut. 6:4.)

We have inherited in our forms of worship many of these elements. We also have psalms or hymns that may be read or sung; we have musical instruments of various kinds, the organ being especially associated with the church, but there is no reason why other instruments would not be equally appropriate. Many sacred works by Bach, Mozart, Handel, and others, regularly performed in European churches, are scored for instruments other than the organ. We ascribe praise; we offer prayers of thanksgiving, petition, and intercession; we state our faith in terms of a creed; we unite in common words spoken in unison; we read from the Bible; and in the sermon we discuss the significance of what is read, in terms of our own time and experience. Is this the correct way to worship?

PROPHETIC PROTEST REGARDING WORSHIP

Because worship tends to take particular forms, it also tends to become perfunctory. The Book of Malachi is a protest against worship that has become mere form. It is addressed to the priests. The prophet says:

> A son honors his father, and a servant his master. If then I am a father, where is my honor? And if I am a master, where is my fear? says the LORD of hosts to you, O priests, who despise my name. You say, "How have we despised thy name?" By offering polluted food upon my altar. And you say, "How have we polluted it?" By thinking that the LORD's table may be despised. When you offer blind animals in sacrifice, is that no evil? And when you offer those that are lame or sick, is that no evil? Present that to your governor; will he be pleased with you or show you favor? says the LORD of hosts. (Mal. 1:6-8.)

The priests are represented as saying, "What a weariness this is" (Mal. 1:13), as though they are tired of the routine of their duties. This is the hazard that worship encounters. If it is not formal, it tends to become disorganized. If it is formal, it tends to become stereotyped, and loses its significance.

Consider Ps. 40:6-8:

> Sacrifice and offering thou dost not desire;
>   but thou hast given me an open ear.

Burnt offering and sin offering
   thou hast not required.
Then I said, " Lo, I come;
   in the roll of the book it is written of me;
I delight to do thy will, O my God;
   thy law is within my heart."

The statement that God does not desire sacrifice is repeated in a number of places.

Hear, O my people, and I will speak,
   O Israel, I will testify against you.
   I am God, your God.
I do not reprove you for your sacrifices;
   your burnt offerings are continually before me.
I will accept no bull from your house,
   nor he-goat from your folds.
For every beast of the forest is mine,
   the cattle on a thousand hills.
I know all the birds of the air,
   and all that moves in the field is mine.

If I were hungry, I would not tell you;
   for the world and all that is in it is mine.
Do I eat the flesh of bulls,
   or drink the blood of goats?
Offer to God a sacrifice of thanksgiving,
   and pay your vows to the Most High;
and call upon me in the day of trouble;
   I will deliver you, and you shall glorify me.
                                (Ps. 50:7-15.)

Here is the plain statement that sacrifices are not really what God wants. He has everything that he needs.

In Ps. 51 we have a very wonderful confession of sin, following which, beginning in v. 15, we read:

O Lord, open thou my lips,
   and my mouth shall show forth thy praise.

> For thou hast no delight in sacrifice;
>> were I to give a burnt offering, thou wouldst not
>> be pleased.
> The sacrifice acceptable to God is a broken spirit;
>> a broken and contrite heart, O God, thou wilt not
>> despise.
>
> (Ps. 51:15-17.)

This is the prophetic doctrine at its best. Interestingly enough, two more verses follow what we have quoted:

> Do good to Zion in thy good pleasure;
>> rebuild the walls of Jerusalem,
> then wilt thou delight in right sacrifices,
>> in burnt offerings and whole burnt offerings;
>> then bulls will be offered on thy altar.
>
> (Ps. 51:18-19.)

This is exactly the opposite of what has preceded it. Obviously, here is an addition to the psalm, made in the time of the exile when the walls of Zion were thrown down. Living when there was no temple, and when priesthood could not perform its former function, the author of these last two verses longed for the good old days and the restoration of the ancient forms. When he read, " Thou hast no delight in sacrifice," he could not believe it, and added that if God would return his people to their land, he would then delight in right sacrifice.

The prophetic protest against formal worship finds classic expression in the first chapter of The Book of Isaiah.

> What to me is the multitude of your sacrifices?
>> says the LORD;
> I have had enough of burnt offerings of rams
>> and the fat of fed beasts;
> I do not delight in the blood of bulls,
>> or of lambs, or of he-goats.
>
> When you come to appear before me,
>> who requires of you

this trampling of my courts?
Bring no more vain offerings;
  incense is an abomination to me.
New moon and sabbath and the calling of assemblies —
  I cannot endure iniquity and solemn assembly.
Your new moons and your appointed feasts
  my soul hates;
they have become a burden to me,
  I am weary of bearing them.
When you spread forth your hands,
  I will hide my eyes from you;
even though you make many prayers,
  I will not listen;
  your hands are full of blood.
Wash yourselves; make yourselves clean;
  remove the evil of your doings
  from before my eyes;
cease to do evil,
  learn to do good;
seek justice,
  correct oppression;
defend the fatherless,
  plead for the widow.

                                        (Isa. 1:11-17.)

The prophetic protest is that liturgical forms are not the true worship of God. Rather, the true worship of God is right conduct. It is doing the right thing, showing compassion for the fatherless and the widow, learning to do good, correcting oppression.

The passage just quoted continues as follows:

Come now, let us reason together,
  says the LORD:
though your sins are like scarlet,
  they shall be as white as snow;
though they are red like crimson,
  they shall become like wool.

> If you are willing and obedient,
>   you shall eat the good of the land;
> But if you refuse and rebel,
>   you shall be devoured by the sword;
>   for the mouth of the LORD has spoken.
>   (Isa. 1:18-20.)

Many a preacher has quoted the first three lines of this passage, and assumed that what is spoken of is a free offer of forgiveness. But these three lines cannot be read without taking into account the last three. It is not so much a promise as an ironic statement. In Hebrew there are three ways of asking a question. One is by employing an interrogatory pronoun or adverb, as in such phrases as " Who is there? " " What is that? " " Where are you? " or " Whom shall I send? " A second way is by prefixing to a statement the particle *ha*, which then turns what follows into a question. This is parallel to the usage in French in which a statement is made and is followed by *n'est-ce pas?* or in German by *nicht wahr?* or in Italian by *non è vero?*

A third way of asking a question, which is also used in English, is by the intonation of the voice. A given statement may be either an assertion of fact or a question, depending on how it is spoken. Consider the following pairs of examples, the first of each pair spoken with a falling inflection, and the second with a rising inflection:

> " You went to visit your cousin last week."
> " You went to visit your cousin last week? "
>
> " My sister is coming tomorrow."
> " My sister is coming tomorrow? "
>
> " That is a new hat you are wearing."
> " That is a new hat you are wearing? "

In all probability, in view of what follows, the verse in Isaiah was spoken with a rising inflection.

Come now, let us argue this out.

The Hebrew word is a legal term.

> If your sins are like scarlet, shall they be white as snow? If
> they are red like crimson, shall they become as wool?

Two alternates are then indicated:

> If you are willing and obedient,
>   you shall eat the good of the land;
> But if you refuse and rebel,
>   you shall be devoured by the sword;
>   for the mouth of the Lord has spoken.

This is no spineless forgiveness. This is a challenge to right living. Unless there is a change to the right kind of conduct, punishment will follow.

The same theme is found in others of the prophetic books.
Jeremiah says:

> Thus says the Lord of hosts, the God of Israel: " Add your
> burnt offerings to your sacrifices, and eat the flesh. For in
> the day that I brought them out of the land of Egypt, I did
> not speak to your fathers or command them concerning burnt
> offerings and sacrifices. But this command I gave them,
> ' Obey my voice, and I will be your God, and you shall be
> my people; and walk in all the way that I command you,
> that it may be well with you.' " (Jer. 7:21-23.)

The prophetic teaching is that true worship of God is in conduct
of life which honors him.

The classic words of Micah are these:

> " With what shall I come before the Lord,
>   and bow myself before God on high?
> Shall I come before him with burnt offerings,
>   with calves a year old?
> Will the Lord be pleased with thousands of rams,
>   with ten thousands of rivers of oil?
> Shall I give my first-born for my transgression,
>   the fruit of my body for the sin of my soul? "

> He has showed you, O man, what is good;
>   and what does the Lord require of you
> but to do justice, and to love kindness,
>   and to walk humbly with your God?
>
>   (Micah 6:6-8.)

Hosea puts it thus:

> For I desire steadfast love and not sacrifice,
>   the knowledge of God, rather than burnt offerings.
>
>   (Hos. 6:6.)

Right conduct, not form and ritual, is the true worship of God.

True Honor of God

The child who would honor his father and mother does so, not by bringing them gifts in profusion, but by being the kind of person of whom they would be proud. The son who honors his parents by being upright, honest, and diligent, and exhibiting the qualities of life that he knows they want, is what they most appreciate. If we are to believe the prophets, the true worship of God today is not by what we say in church, or what we sing in church, or even the fact that we come to church. It is being the kind of people of whom he would be proud. It is being the kind of children who please their Father because of what they are.

This leads us to say that the true way to honor God is by the way men live together with one another. Religion, for Jesus, was a way of living with men as well as with God. One grows out of the other. With God, men were to live as children, in trust, in devotion, in unity of spirit. The mark of the child was the Spirit of the Father in him. But this Spirit of the Father must be shown, and could only be shown, by his children in relation to their brothers. In the human family, a harmonious relationship between brothers and sisters is the circumstance that most of all brings joy to parents. A happy and harmonious family is the supreme joy of parenthood. It is what parents strive to bring about, most of all, because it is the indication of the effectiveness of their unselfish example, the efficacy of their teaching and instruction, and the result of their provision of individual liberty under wise supervision. Affection toward parents is reflected in affection between the younger members of the human family.

So the dual command of love toward God and love toward man, to which Jesus reduced all commands, becomes one rule, one spirit, by which man is to live. To be a brother to men in the spirit of the common Father is a very simple rule of life, but its scope is wide and its standard is high. It includes all men, good and evil, black and white, near and far. Of course, Jesus recognized the differences between evil and good men, between Jew and Samaritan. But in his conversation with the Samaritan woman (John 4:7-26), there is no hint that he thought of her otherwise than as a person, in no sense inferior to other persons. When Jesus cleansed ten lepers, and instructed them to go and show themselves to the priests, it is said that only one turned back to give thanks to Jesus, and the comment is added, " Now he was a Samaritan " (Luke 17:16). In answer to the lawyer's question, " And who is my neighbor? " (Luke 10:29), Jesus related the parable in which the hero is the good Samaritan.

The point is that what people of diverse backgrounds demonstrate is what they have in common. Each is a man, with a value outweighing a whole world of things (Mark 8:36-37). There is not one that is not the object of God's love and care. Heaven rejoices when one wandering child of God comes back. Anger, scorn, contempt, the hard and unforgiving spirit — these are sins that call forth the strongest denunciations of our Lord.

The demand of Jesus in relation to man's life with men is plain. First of all, there must be reverence for humanity in the person of every human being. Second, there must be the spirit of forgiveness or no forgiveness can be expected for us (Matt. 6:15). Third, there must be goodwill, not just love as a vague sentimentality but as the positive and active will seeking the good of others. Finally, there is the demand of service and sacrifice. If men can display such aspects of the teaching of Jesus, making them concrete and objective in their relations with others, they will demonstrate that the family of God can be like the ideal human family. Of such relationship among children, a parent would be most proud. He would be honored by such a family.

This kind of honor is not done best in solitude. There are those who aver that they can worship just as well in the forest or on the mountain, at the seashore or on the golf course, as they can in church. We not infrequently hear the question: "Is it not possible to be a good Christian outside the church? If I love my neighbor, deal honestly, and practice the Golden Rule, can I not be as good a Christian outside as inside the church?" In view of what we have been saying, this is probably the case. But there is another consideration. When we camp out in the woods in summer, it is traditional to build a campfire in the evening, and sit and watch it. There it sparkles, crackles, and burns briskly, and a twig snaps out and lands to one side. It burns brightly for some moments, and then it goes out. It would not have gone out if it had stayed in the fire. This could be a parable of the Christian outside the church. It is possible to live according to the gospel in solitude, but the warmth of others who are on fire with the good news of Christ speaks for the necessity of Christian community. Corporate worship is part of the honoring of God, though it is not the end in itself. Corporate worship should be one of the things that help us to be the kind of persons who truly honor the Father who is in heaven.

The conclusion, therefore, is that worship and righteousness go together. One is not possible without the other. Both of them belong in the experience of the honest Christian.

IV · *Law and Gospel*

We turn now to the question of the requirements of the Christian faith. Every major religion indicates certain modes of conduct that are considered important because they are right. To be a good Muslim, one must conform to five acts or assertions. One must daily affirm that there is no God but Allah, and Muhammad is his prophet. Five times daily one must pray in the direction of Mecca. To give alms is a requirement. One must observe the fast of Ramadan. And, once in his lifetime, the Muslim must make a pilgrimage to Mecca. These are the requirements of Islam.

Judaism through the generations has emphasized conformity to the law as the essence of righteousness. This involves forms of worship, prayer, Sabbath observance, and other elements. So, also, Christian tradition lays stress on both faith and conduct. Jesus summed it up in the great commandment:

> You shall love the Lord your God with all your heart, and with all your soul, and with all your mind. This is the great and first commandment. And a second is like it, You shall love your neighbor as yourself. On these two commandments depend all the law and the prophets. (Matt. 22:37-40.)

A further statement is found in the Golden Rule:

> Whatever you wish that men would do to you, do so to them; for this is the law and the prophets. (Matt. 7:12.)

The Letter of James discusses the relation of faith to works:

> But some one will say, "You have faith and I have works." Show me your faith apart from your works, and I by my works will show you my faith. (James 2:18.)

The position of Paul is that we are sanctified by faith. To King Agrippa he told of his conversion on the Damascus road and of his call to go to the Gentiles

> to open their eyes, that they may turn from darkness to light and from the power of Satan to God, that they may receive forgiveness of sins and a place among those who are sanctified by faith in me. (Acts 26:18.)

He enlarges upon this theme in his letters, notably in Romans. Here he says that the agent of sanctification is the Holy Spirit (Rom. 15:16).

THE MEANING OF SANCTIFICATION

" To sanctify " is " to make holy," " to declare holy," or " to regard as holy." A first usage is found in the Old Testament, where the commandment is to "remember the sabbath day, to keep it holy " (Ex. 20:8). It was to be separated from other days and set apart for the honor of God. So also the vessels of the sanctuary were separated from common usage and consecrated to the service of God. We read in II Chron. 7:7 that

> Solomon consecrated the middle of the court that was before the house of the LORD; for there he offered the burnt offering and the fat of the peace offerings, because the bronze altar Solomon had made could not hold the burnt offering and the cereal offering and the fat.

This same usage is found in the first petition of the Lord's Prayer:

> Hallowed be thy name. (Matt. 6:9.)

To hallow God's name is neither to make it holy nor to consecrate it, but simply to recognize and declare it such.

A second usage is that of consecration. This is accomplished by ritual. By special symbolical action that which is separated from common use and dedicated to religious purposes is given a new, though conventional, character. The priesthood acquired this ceremonial holiness by consecration (Ex. 28:41; 29:9). So also the altar is set apart for its special function by consecration (Ex. 29:37), as well as the Tabernacle furniture and sacrificial utensils (Ex. 40:9-10). The Levites are to be distinguished from the rest of the tribes by such consecration to the Lord's service (Num. 8:14-17), and of course the Temple is sanctified and set apart when it is completed, as a special sign and demonstration of its unique position in the worship of the nation (I Kings 9:3). According to Lev. 11:44, the whole people is to be consecrated:

> For I am the LORD your God; consecrate yourselves therefore, and be holy, for I am holy.

This is assumed also in Num. 11:18.

The prophet Jeremiah records that at his call the Lord indicated that Jeremiah had previously been set apart by consecration for the task assigned to him:

> Now the word of the LORD came to me saying,
>
>> "Before I formed you in the womb I knew you,
>> and before you were born I consecrated you;
>> I appointed you a prophet to the nations."
>>
>> (Jer. 1:4-5.)

It is only in the New Testament that a third usage is found. In this sense "to sanctify" is "to make inwardly whole." It appears first in Paul's teaching. In the Gospels, no mention is made of inward sanctification. In the utterances of Jesus, "to sanctify" is "to consecrate." It is the Temple that sanctifies the gold, and the altar that sanctifies the gift (Matt. 23:17, 19). Paul, however, passes to an ethical sense.

> For this is the will of God, your sanctification. (I Thess. 4:3.)

The verses that follow show that he included in his thought the control and direction of the body in purity by the Spirit, the putting off of sin, and the putting on of holiness.

God's Spirit, working outward from within, constitutes the essence of sanctification. The whole person is thus sanctified:

> If the dough offered as first fruits is holy, so is the whole
> lump; and if the root is holy, so are the branches. (Rom.
> 11:16.)

Sanctification is for Paul not a simple act, nor yet a process that
must be completed before it can be strictly called by that name.
It is complete at the outset. Yet it is a process that admits of
growth and increasingly nearer approximation to its ideal completion. In the Old Testament, sanctification was static in form.
In Paul's use it becomes dynamic. In the Old Testament, it was
the act of consecration that made the person or object holy. In
Paul's usage, it is understood as conformity to God's character,
rather than separation to his service. Whenever, therefore, the
thought reverts to the static aspect of the conception, sanctification appears as a thing already complete. Hence believers are
holy. They are saints (Rom. 12:13; II Cor. 1:1; Eph. 1:1; etc.).
But whenever the idea points to the dynamic or growing side of
the notion, sanctification is progressive. It indicates that the Spirit
of God is progressively changing the sinner into increasingly perfect conformity to God's whole image. It is the mark of the
mature Christian. This is by the grace of God:

> Therefore, since we are justified by faith, we have peace with
> God through our Lord Jesus Christ. Through him we have
> obtained access to this grace in which we stand. (Rom. 5:1-2.)

In the next chapter he asserts:

> For sin will have no dominion over you, since you are not
> under law but under grace. (Rom. 6:14.)

To the Galatians he wrote:

> We ourselves, who are Jews by birth and not Gentile sinners,
> yet who know that a man is not justified by works of the
> law but through faith in Jesus Christ, even we have believed
> in Christ Jesus, in order to be justified by faith in Christ,
> and not by works of the law, because by works of the law
> shall no one be justified. (Gal. 2:15-16.)

If it is true that no one is justified by works of the law, what shall we say of the relation of law to gospel? Through the years this has led to a downgrading of the law in Christian eyes. We are freed from the law in order to live under the gospel.

The Biblical Usage of the Word "Law"

But this is too easy an answer. It results from a misunderstanding of the nature of the law. The Hebrew word translated "law" is *torah*. It is from a root that means "to direct" or "to instruct." *Torah* is properly "instruction" or "direction." "Gospel" is from the Old English "godspel" and translates the Greek *euangelion*. It means essentially "good news." It is the good news of Christ. It is cause for rejoicing. Let us consider the relation of instruction or direction to the good news of Christ. We may distinguish several different usages of the idea of law, so far as the Bible is concerned. The word may designate the first five books of the Bible, known as the Pentateuch. The well-known designation of the Bible in Hebrew was Law, Prophets, and Writings. The Writings were also called The Psalms because of the fact that The Psalms was the first book in the third division. Our Lord spoke of "everything written about me in the law of Moses and the prophets and the psalms" (Luke 24:44). But the word "law" may refer also to the entire Old Testament. John 12:34 asserts that the crowd said:

> We have heard from the law that the Christ remains for ever. How can you say that the Son of man must be lifted up?

In John 15:25, Jesus is quoted as saying:

> It is to fulfil the word that is written in their law, "They hated me without a cause." (Cf. Ps. 35:19; 69:4.)

These are quotations from the Writings, which are termed "law."

The word may apply also to the Ten Commandments. Paul wrote that

> I should not have known what it is to covet if the law had not said, "You shall not covet." (Rom. 7:7.)

More generally, Paul uses the word to designate the entire Mosaic system, which extended from earliest times until the Christian gospel. In Gal. 3:17 he speaks of "the law, which came four hundred and thirty years afterward," by which he means the system of Mosaic law, and not simply the Ten Commandments. Closely related to this is the usage that employs the term as referring to moral law in general. The great commandment sums up the moral law. Again, the word may designate a principle, a uniformly acting influence. Paul writes:

> On what principle? On the principle of works? No, but on the principle of faith. For we hold that a man is justified by faith apart from works of law. (Rom. 3:27-28.)

The word "law" also has both a general and a specific usage. We speak today of "going to law," by which we mean legal procedure in whatever form may be contemporary. So Paul writes:

> Do you not know, brethren — for I am speaking to those who know the law — that the law is binding on a person only during his life? Thus a married woman is bound by law to her husband as long as he lives. (Rom. 7:1-2.)

But the word may apply also to particular precepts or regulations. This usage is reflected in the words of the Jews:

> We have a law, and by that law he ought to die, because he has made himself the Son of God. (John 19:7; cf. Lev. 24:16; Matt. 26:63-66.)

It is therefore obvious that to contrast law and gospel involves a rather delicate definition of terminology. The Biblical usage of the term "law" requires discernment and understanding if we are not to make a mistake. In order to gain perspective, let us take some time to discover how the Old Testament law came into being.

Old Testament law represents a long period of development and growth. It originated in family and tribal relationships.

Wherever people must live together, certain patterns of conduct develop and certain customs receive general approval so that society may be orderly and the individual member protected. Many of the regulations under which Western civilization lives go back in their origins to Roman law. It is truly said that the great legacy the Romans left to posterity was their regard for law. Some of our American regulations find their origin in English common law. But we are indebted in considerable measure to the Old Testament as well.

CASUISTIC AND APODICTIC LAW

Scholars distinguish two kinds of regulation so far as the Pentateuch is concerned. Old Testament laws of one kind are termed " casuistic law," and another kind is commonly designated as " apodictic law." Casuistic law is what is found, for example, in Ex., chs. 21 to 23. It is what is formulated by experience in actual cases. The correct way to act is determined on the basis of practice. Specific cases are brought, specific instances are cited, and the priest, or judge, tries to determine the proper response to the situation.

Consider Ex. 21:2-6:

> When you buy a Hebrew slave, he shall serve six years, and in the seventh he shall go out free, for nothing. If he comes in single, he shall go out single; if he comes in married, then his wife shall go out with him. If his master gives him a wife and she bears him sons or daughters, the wife and her children shall be her master's and he shall go out alone. But if the slave plainly says, " I love my master, my wife, and my children; I will not go out free," then his master shall bring him to God [i.e., to the priest], and he shall bring him to the door or the doorpost; and his master shall bore his ear through with an awl; and he shall serve him for life.

Here we note a series of different situations, in which different procedures are to be followed, according to the circumstances.

Again, we read:

> Whoever strikes a man so that he dies shall be put to death.
> But if he did not lie in wait for him, but God let ·him fall
> into his hand, then I will appoint for you a place to which
> he may flee. But if a man willfully attacks another to kill
> him treacherously, you shall take him from my altar, that
> he may die. (Ex. 21:12-14.)

This distinguishes murder from manslaughter. The place of
refuge available to the manslayer is not valid for the murderer.
Again we note that, according to the circumstances, the law is
variously applied.

Another example is this:

> When an ox gores a man or a woman to death, the ox shall
> be stoned, and its flesh shall not be eaten; but the owner of
> the ox shall be clear. But if the ox has been accustomed to
> gore in the past, and its owner has been warned but has not
> kept it in, and it kills a man or a woman, the ox shall be
> stoned, and its owner also shall be put to death. (Ex.
> 21:28-29.)

These are examples of casuistic law. They grow out of specific
cases, specific instances, and indicate how, under differing circumstances, men and women can live together in order and harmony.

The other type of law discerned by scholars is termed apodictic
law. As recognized from its Greek origin, what is apodictic is
" said forth " or " spoken out." It is a pronouncement in principle.
Perhaps the best examples of this kind of law might be the Ten
Commandments:

> God spoke all these words, saying, . . .
> " You shall have no other gods before me.
> " You shall not make for yourself a graven image. . . .
> " You shall not take the name of the LORD your
>   God in vain. . . .
> " Remember the sabbath day, to keep it holy. . . .
> " Honor your father and your mother. . . .
> " You shall not kill."
>
> (Ex. 20:1-13 ff.)

These are pronouncements in principle. They do not grow out of legal procedure.

Casuistic and apodictic law are, therefore, instances of legal enactment in the strict sense. But how much of the Pentateuch consists of this kind of regulation? *Torah* means "instruction" or "direction," as we have seen. Let us consider the Pentateuch as a whole with this in mind.

THE CONTENT OF THE BOOK OF GENESIS

The first eleven chapters of Genesis are concerned with beginnings. Here are the accounts of creation: how the world was created by the word of God, the story of the man in the garden, the first sin, the first murder. There follows a genealogical table of ancient times, then the account of Noah and the great Flood, and a list of the descendants of Noah. Finally, in ch. 11, is the account of the Tower of Babel. These accounts are not history, in a real sense. That is to say, they are not so much events that occurred at particular moments as they are representations of the problems of human society. They may properly be called the parables of Genesis.

We have already examined the accounts of creation. Let us look at the story of the Tower of Babel. Is this really an event that took place in Babylon? The Tower of Babel is evidently meant to designate the temple tower of Babylon, the ziggurat, or mound, on which stood the temple sacred to Bel-Merodach. We are told that the world was unified, and that men said, "Come, let us build ourselves a city, and a tower with its top in the heavens, and let us make a name for ourselves, lest we be scattered abroad upon the face of the whole earth" (Gen. 11:4). We are not supposed to understand that they intended to climb into heaven upon the tower. It was to reach the sky — to be a skyscraper. It was to be a monument to human achievement, and they went to work with a will. However, as they neared completion of the project, it is said that they became unable to understand one another. Their language was confused, so they could not get along with one another and they were dispersed to the ends of the earth.

There is profound insight in this story. Differences of language have always been a source of trouble, the symbol and accentuation of division, strangeness, suspicion, and hostility. In human pride, men seek to build a structure that will surpass anything previously known. In spite of this achievement, they do not understand one another, and reach a point where they can no longer cooperate. This is certainly a picture of our world. We, today, with all our knowledge, our technology, our science, our education, our background in history, our appreciation of the arts and of the world, still find ourselves at odds with one another. We are still confused. The word "confused" in Genesis is a pun on the name "Babylon": in Hebrew the word for Babylon is *Babel,* and the verb "to confuse" is *bālal.* It is as though we might say that nuclear fusion brings human confusion. Genesis represents man as self-asserting, believing that by his own devices he can reach the pinnacle of coveted importance, but in reality impotent to get along with himself.

It is in ways like these that we may regard the first eleven chapters of Genesis as parables. Then, beginning with the twelfth chapter, we find the patriarchal narratives. These are the accounts of Abraham, Isaac, and Jacob, their wanderings and their activities, told in chs. 12 to 36, together with some interspersed material, such as genealogies of the kings of Edom (ch. 36). Generally, they are the remembered accounts of the ancestors of the Hebrew people. Finally, in chs. 37 to 50, we find the story of Joseph, sold into Egypt by his brothers, rising to a position of authority, showing mercy to his brothers, inviting them and all their families down into Egypt, where they settle and prosper. Genesis thus ends. Yet not one regulation or enactment is found. The accounts are religious teaching: they are direction, or instruction, but they are not legal enactment. They are *torah.*

THE CONTENT OF THE BOOK OF EXODUS

The book of Exodus begins by relating how the descendants of Jacob multiplied in the land, and then states that there arose a new king over Egypt, who did not know Joseph. The people were oppressed, Moses received a call to lead them out, and there is an account of the ten plagues suffered by the Egyptians. The exodus took place, and the people escaped, only to be pursued by Pharaoh and his chariots. They arrived at the Red Sea, or, more properly, the Sea of Reeds, for the Hebrew phrase indicates a reedy marsh, which was probably somewhere north of the Gulf of Suez. There a great deliverance took place, remembered in succeeding centuries as an act of God.

Many modern scholars are of the opinion that what really took place was an unexpected military victory by the men of Israel over the Egyptians. The account in Ex., chs. 14 and 15, is edited from composite sources, and the nucleus appears not to have been the idea of a wind blowing the water back or of walls of water standing congealed as the Israelites passed through "on dry ground" (Ex. 14:22), but of a military encounter in which Israel defeated the pursuing chariotry of Pharaoh. This is attested by the repeated use of military terms. "The people of Israel went up out of the land of Egypt equipped for battle." (Ex. 13:18.) This would be meaningless in the account unless a battle ensued. The military term "encamp" is used in Ex. 13:20, also in ch. 14:2, 9, while the term "host," meaning "army," is used in ch. 13:19-20, where it clearly designates the armies of both Egypt and Israel. In ch. 14:14, it is said that "the Lord will fight for you," that is, will win the battle, as is said elsewhere in the Old Testament. When the Lord "discomfited the host of the Egyptians" (Ex. 14:24), "to throw into confusion" is the word characteristically used when Israel's army was victorious. (Cf. Ex. 23:27; Josh. 10:10; Judg. 4:15; I Sam. 7:10.)

It would appear that what actually happened was that Israel retreated into the marshy ground near the Sea of Reeds, that Pharaoh's chariots attempted to follow, expecting an easy victory, but that the wheels sank into the ooze,

> clogging their chariot wheels so that they drove heavily; and the Egyptians said, "Let us flee from before Israel; for the Lord fights for them against the Egyptians." (Ex. 14:25.)

The major weapon on which the Egyptians had relied became unmaneuverable and completely ineffective. Apparently, the

Egyptians' inability to move in the mud made them sitting targets for the Hebrew archers. Thus

> the LORD routed the Egyptians in the midst of the sea. (Ex. 14:27.)

The victory of the Lord in Israel's battle is celebrated in the Song of Miriam:

> Sing to the LORD, for he has triumphed gloriously;
> the horse and his rider he has thrown into the sea.
> > (Ex. 15:21; cf. 15:1.)

This is a victory song, evidently composed to celebrate a military triumph. In succeeding generations, probably, the elements of the wind and the dividing of the waters were added to become part of the glorious saga of deliverance. The whole Song of Moses, in Ex., ch. 15, is full of symbolic and metaphorical expressions, enlarging upon these themes. Thus we have the record of the deliverance of Israel from those who oppressed them.

The people made their way to the base of Mt. Sinai, and while they waited below, Moses is said to have climbed into the mountain, and ch. 20 records that "God spoke all these words, saying, 'I am the LORD your God, who brought you out of the land of Egypt, out of the house of bondage. You shall have no other gods before me.'" The first enactment that we find in the Pentateuch is the apodictic law in Ex. 20:3. The rest of the Ten Commandments follow.

The next chapter begins the listing of casuistic law, which we considered earlier. Then the narrative is resumed, and the remainder of the book of Exodus is largely the section in which divine revelation to Moses describes the Tabernacle and its furnishings, and the incident of the golden calf is recorded. Finally, several chapters relate the construction and furnishing of the Tabernacle, and Exodus comes to a conclusion. Regarding the book as a whole, we note that a few chapters are enactments, but most of the book is narrative, as was Genesis. When we translate *torah* by "law," we should note that instruction may be by example as well as by precept. The traditions about Abraham, Isaac,

Jacob, Joseph, Moses, and those associated with them, are just as much torah as the sections that contain legal enactments.

Leviticus, Numbers, and Deuteronomy

An examination of Leviticus discloses that here are indeed regulations, mostly of a religious nature, relating to proper conduct of sacrifice, tithes, vows, and the like, though the section beginning in ch. 18 is more properly a sermon put into the mouth of Moses. The book of Numbers contains both narrative and laws, while Deuteronomy is largely in the form of three sermons attributed to Moses, and carrying back to him the great teachings of the prophets of the eighth and seventh centuries before Christ. It is an attempt to portray, on the basis of the covenant, how men should love the Lord their God, and how they should live together in response to him. It recalls the experience at Sinai, relating it to settled communal living under the Davidic dynasty.

Thus we see that by calling the Pentateuch " law," and supposing it therefore to be primarily legal regulations, then contrasting law and gospel, setting rules over against Christian freedom, we are in danger of misunderstanding the true significance of the law. We need to have a higher view of the Old Testament law, for the torah is not really so much the regulations themselves as it is the spirit in which the regulations are set forth.

Israel Under Foreign Domination

Later developments brought legalism to the fore. The Northern Kingdom was overcome by the Assyrians in 721 B.C., and Judah lost her independence in 597 B.C., when Nebuchadnezzar captured Jerusalem. First, they were subjects of Babylon, then Babylon was conquered by the Persians in 539, and Palestine became a Persian province and remained so for two hundred years. Then came Alexander the Great, who conquered the Persians in 333–331 B.C. For ten years he ruled the then known world. In 323 B.C. he died, and tradition has it that he wept that there were no more worlds to conquer. He was a great administrator from a secular point of view. He believed that it was incumbent upon the Greeks to extend Greek culture throughout the world, so that other peoples might enjoy the benefits that the Greeks had received through their philosophers, their teachers, and their art. This should become the heritage of the rest of the world.

But with the death of Alexander in 323 B.C., his empire split into four parts — no one person was able to succeed him, and there came into being the four so-called Hellenistic kingdoms, under the Diadochi. Ptolemy became ruler of Egypt, Syria was under Seleucus, Cassander ruled Macedonia, while Thrace and Asia Minor went to Lysimachus. From 323 to 197 B.C., Palestine was under the control of the Ptolemaic dynasty of Egypt, and from 197 to 142 B.C. was subject to the house of Seleucus and attached to Syria. These rulers were Greeks. They considered themselves obligated to help their subjects see the light in terms of Greek culture.

We may easily imagine what this policy meant to the followers of Moses. Here was an obvious attempt to replace the heritage of Israel with an alien culture. Several parties came into being among the Jews, each with its own attitude as to how to respond to this kind of situation. There were, first of all, the Sadducees, whose name is derived from the Hebrew word for "righteous." This party was willing to come to terms with the Greeks, and favored taking over the best in Greek culture, combining it with the most significant in their own heritage. But the Pharisees, deriving their name from the Hebrew verb "to separate," avowed that they would have nothing to do with Greek ways, since this would endanger what made their own inheritance distinctive. To them, the law was all-important. They accepted its teachings and its regulations, and enlarged upon them. They insisted that they could live with this in the midst of a Greek society, and yet maintain their distinctive Hebrew tradition. There came into being, both in Palestine and in Babylonia, two works known as "Talmud," from a root that means "teaching." These were extended commentaries on the law, intended to make the regulations specific in terms of everyday living.

How Shall the Sabbath Day Be Kept Holy?

For example, if one is to "remember the sabbath day, to keep it holy" (Ex. 20:8), what does this mean in practical terms? The scribes became specific. They devised a Sabbath-day's journey (Acts 1:12), which was the distance of 2,000 cubits, based on Josh. 3:4. To travel farther than this would be work, and was not permissible. Then they devised a way to circumvent this, and double the distance, for if one deposited food at a distance of 2,000 cubits, one might designate the spot as his temporary home, travel to that spot, and then travel an equal distance beyond.

As for cooking on the Sabbath, that was prohibited, for it was work. Suppose one prepared food the day before. Would it be permissible to eat it on the Sabbath? The answer was affirmative, for no work was done on the Sabbath. Suppose that one prepared food the day before, and laid a fire under it. Would it be permissible to kindle it on the Sabbath? The answer was negative, for kindling fire would be work. Suppose that the food was thus prepared, the fire laid, and owing to the fact that hot coals were in the ashes, it should happen to catch fire on the Sabbath. Should one put it out? No, for extinguishing the fire would be work. Would it be lawful to eat food thus cooked? Evidently this is the Lord's will, so the food may be eaten.

It is not hard to see that this kind of legalism became ridiculous. Yet it represented the Pharisaic mind. In modern times there are those whose attitude toward the law is similar. The Christian Lord's Day is not the continuation of the Jewish Sabbath. They are two different things, from two different origins. The early Christians, remembering the day of the resurrection, came together on the first day of the week. This was not the Sabbath, which was the seventh day, but an entirely different commemoration. Jewish Christians at first observed the Sabbath, but they also remembered the resurrection on the first day of the week. Gentile Christians did not observe the Sabbath, but they did observe the Lord's Day, which became an analogous institution.

The Puritans understood that the Lord's Day was the Sabbath, and called it such. Then they devised regulations — the so-called blue laws — to make the observance legal and compulsory. How can one apply such regulations in a day like ours? The steel industry has great furnaces that run seven days a week. They cannot be shut down one day a week, for it would take too long to restart them. They run continuously for months, until it is necessary to shut them down and rebuild them. Someone must be there day and night to tend them. How could a Sabbath rule be made to apply in this instance? To take another example, in a day when frozen foods are commonplace, electric freezers must be in continuous operation to preserve them. This means that the electric power plants that supply the energy must operate seven days a week. It would be simply unreasonable to shut them down on the Sabbath. To attempt to codify Sabbath regulations in a Talmud for our time would be a futile undertaking.

It was this kind of regulation that Jesus had in mind when the scribes and Pharisees asked him:

" Why do your disciples not live according to the tradition of the elders, but eat with hands defiled? " And he said to them, . . . "You leave the commandment of God, and hold fast the tradition of men. . . . You have a fine way of rejecting the commandment of God, in order to keep your tradition! " (Mark 7:5-6, 8-9.)

When Jesus denounced legalism, he was not denouncing the law. His remarks concerned the way in which men regarded that law. His denunciation of the scribes and the Pharisees focused on their literal minds, which could see nothing but legal enactments. Elsewhere it is recorded that on another occasion he said:

Woe to you, scribes and Pharisees, hypocrites! for you tithe mint and dill and cummin, and have neglected the weightier matters of the law, justice and mercy and faith; these you ought to have done, without neglecting the others. You blind guides, straining out a gnat and swallowing a camel! (Matt. 23:23-24.)

Here we have the clue to Jesus' attitude toward the law. He declared that meticulous observance of detailed enactment really misses the point. He respected the deep and lasting significance of the law, for it was not in fact enactment but teaching. On the occasion when Jesus healed a man afflicted with dropsy on the Sabbath, he was roundly criticized by those with legalistic minds. He retorted:

> " Which of you, having an ass or an ox that has fallen into a well, will not immediately pull him out on a sabbath day? " And they could not reply to this. (Luke 14:5-6.)

His basic position is summed up in his statement:

> Think not that I have come to abolish the law and the prophets; I have come not to abolish them but to fulfil them. For truly, I say to you, till heaven and earth pass away, not an iota, not a dot, will pass from the law until all is accomplished. (Matt. 5:17-18.)

THE CHRISTIAN GOSPEL IN RELATION TO INHERITED TRADITION

How does the gospel relate itself to this kind of teaching? The principle is that in the gospel is freedom from regulation. Jesus said, " I came that they may have life, and have it abundantly " (John 10:10). He and his disciples were not concerned with regulations. True, he went, as was his custom, into the synagogue on the Sabbath day; he participated in the worship in the Temple, but he considered these services in terms of principle rather than of fulfilling of requirements. The gospel does not turn its back on the great religious principles of the past. It fulfills the principles inherent in the ancient faith. It teaches freedom, but it does not teach irresponsibility.

In every human activity there are two aspects of endeavor. On the one hand is the past, which represents experience. On the other hand is the future, which represents our goals. It will not do to ignore the experience of the past, for if the future is to have significance, it will grow out of the past. Continuity is the key to the future.

A mountain climber needs two feet. With one he holds the

ground he has gained; with the other he reaches forward and takes another step toward new heights. Neither foot can be dispensed with. With only one foot, he might hold what he has achieved, but there he would remain. If he wished to progress, he would have to hop or jump, an unstable process, to say the least. He would have to lose his connection with the past, and the uncertainty of a new foothold would be greatly increased. So also, in the Christian life, two things are necessary. There must be an element of conservatism, in its best sense, that holds fast to what has been, and there must also be an element of progressivism into the future, moving forward to realize new goals.

The difference between law and gospel is the difference between the system and the individual. Law exemplified the system whereby the sons of Israel participated in the great heritage of the past, whereas Jesus taught that every individual is a child of God, with the possibility of moving into areas far beyond anything their fathers have experienced. It was not enough to maintain the inheritance of preceding generations. Jesus pointed to new possibilities of response in days to come.

> You have heard that it was said, " You shall love your neighbor and hate your enemy." But I say to you, Love your enemies and pray for those who persecute you, so that you may be sons of your Father who is in heaven. . . . You, therefore, must be perfect, as your heavenly Father is perfect. (Matt. 5:43-45, 48.)

It is not sufficient to hold on to what has been. Conservatism has its place, but progressivism will make the future.

A great deal is being said in these days about ethics and morality. Let us remind ourselves of the origin of these words. " Ethics " is derived from the Greek word *ēthos,* which is the word for custom, usage, or character. Ethics describes the way people act or respond. "Morality" is from the Latin word *mores,* which means custom, habit, manner, or way of acting. Mores are the ways in which people customarily act. Ethics and morality are consequently the ways in which people act or respond under given circumstances. What is customary in various parts of the world is considered the right and normal course of action there. It is thought proper to live in accordance with the accepted norms of the society of which one is a member.

When the Puritans settled in the New World, they demanded conformity to their standards. One who was unwilling to conform was obliged to go elsewhere. William Penn and his Quaker compatriots in Pennsylvania set their standards of community and personal action. Roger Williams, a Baptist, found it necessary to leave Massachusetts and find a new location, settling in what is now Rhode Island. When John Calvin became the ruler of Geneva, he set the standards of morality and religion. Those who would not conform were under duress. During the Reformation, the community in which one lived determined the social norms of belief and action. Persecution lay in store for those who were unable or unwilling to conform.

We should probably do well to consider to what extent we are bound by custom and habit. English law was based in part on Roman law, but there was also a vast reservoir of unwritten law which we call common law, on the basis of which a great many of our present-day attitudes depend. Thus it is that custom determines many of our decisions and responses.

But our day is witnessing rebellion against authority and custom. College students, teen-agers, and young people of minority groups characteristically reject conformity. By their dress, their hair styling — or lack of styling — and their habits, they seek to indicate their break with what is commonly accepted in society. To many of the older generation, such rejection of authority is deeply disturbing. So, also, for many, is the so-called " new morality." Yet a number of writers have come to a defense of the new ethics, and question whether there are absolutes in matters of conduct. They contend that right and wrong may vary according to context. What is right in one situation may be wrong in another. They aver that particular decisions as to how to act must be made in the light of conditions of the moment. They appeal for responsible action on the basis of Christian freedom, placing emphasis on the person rather than on the system. They understand this to be the logical and natural application of the gospel with its emphasis on freedom and the development of the abundant life.

Freedom always involves risk. There is always the chance that wrong decisions may be made. But the position of the gospel is that it is worth the risk. Only so can mature persons develop. Parents make decisions for young children to protect them. Parents decide when the child shall eat, when he shall sleep, what he shall wear, where he shall go. But these decisions are made for the immature. Eventually the child is taught to make his own decisions. As he grows, more and more freedom is given to him so that he may learn. Of course this involves risk. Nevertheless, it is part of growing up, and the goal of all child education is to produce mature persons capable of making decisions. Only so does character develop. This is the message of the Christian gospel. It is the continuity of the teaching of the law, but it emphasizes freedom rather than conformity. It is the fulfillment of the law.

V · *Separation and Reconciliation*

If the gospel means liberty, as it does — that is, freedom from regulation — the possibility of making a mistake is introduced. We noted in the preceding chapter that as a child grows up he is given more and more freedom to make decisions. The process of maturing means ever-increasing liberty of action. Wrong decisions may be made, however, with inevitable consequences. Of course, all too frequently this is what happens.

It is exactly parallel to the Christian life. God the Father has brought his children into the world, and he desires that they become mature Christians. Whereas there was a time when he led them very carefully, his goal is that they may have perfect liberty, freedom to choose the right way.

> Now the Lord is the Spirit, and where the Spirit of the Lord is, there is freedom. (II Cor. 3:17.)

> For freedom Christ has set us free; stand fast therefore, and do not submit again to a yoke of slavery. (Gal. 5:1.)

> For you were called to freedom, brethren; only do not use your freedom as an opportunity for the flesh, but through love be servants of one another. (Gal. 5:13.)

> So speak and so act as those who are to be judged under the law of liberty. (James 2:12.)

There is a verse in the book of Proverbs that is often quoted:

> Train up a child in the way he should go,
> and when he is old he will not depart from it.
> (Prov. 22:6.)

This seems to say to the ordinary reader that " as the twig is bent, the tree inclines." That is, start the child in the way in which you want him to go, and he will continue along that line when supervision ceases. But that is not what the verse means. That is indoctrination, not education, and would mean that we are making the child's plans for him, determining his choices for him. It suggests that his elders plot his course and when he matures, he will follow along that course. The Hebrew does not mean this, for literally it reads:

Train up a child according to his way,
and when he is old, he will not turn aside.

The author of the proverb was indeed wise and really meant that a child should be trained "according to his way." What, really, is "his way"? It depends on what kind of person he is. What is his personality, his talent, his ability? Is he clever with his hands, or ingenious with his head? Is he an activist, or is he introspective? Many parents insist on training their children in ways that are not suitable to them. They would like to have a professional man when they really have an artisan. They may wish to see their son follow his father, and continue the father's business, not recognizing that the son is an intellectual genius. They send their child to college when he should go to trade school, or vice versa. Then, when he matures and realizes that he is not suited for the career for which his parents have attempted to educate him, he turns to something else.

To train a child "according to his way" means to train him according to his abilities. If we can discover a child's potential, let us train him for it, and when he is old, he will not turn aside. This is the true meaning of education, which by its etymology means to "lead out" what is within. Education leads out what is within the child. Fortunate indeed is the parent or teacher who can discover the child's inclination and bring it to maturity.

Our purpose is, therefore, to give young people freedom so that they may find themselves. But this involves freedom to make a mistake. It is the calculated risk that we take.

Evidently in God's providential creation of this world, he has given men many abilities and many opportunities, then has set them free to make the most of their opportunities. Our responsibility is to train ourselves in the way in which we should go. Our duty is to discover what talents, abilities, and qualifications have been put in our possession, and to use them for the honor and worship of the Creator. In setting us free, God has taken a calculated risk that we can make a mistake. Of course, this is the sorry course of human history.

When a child makes a mistake, what is the result so far as the family is concerned? What he has done is contrary to the wishes of his parents, or is to the disadvantage of his brother or sister. The result is estrangement, tension, and separation. A barrier arises where there was none before. A strain comes into being between one person and another. Similarly, when man makes a mistake, there comes estrangement between him and his Creator. Separation from God is the result of man's doing the wrong thing. A broken relationship comes into being between man and God. It is the result of man's willfulness, and his propensity to err. The Biblical word for this is " sin."

THE BIBLICAL CONCEPT OF SIN

" Sin " is not a popular word today. We do not like to talk about sin, and psychiatrists have other words for it. They speak of a guilt complex, and this is nothing else than what results from sin. The fact is there, whether we use one word or another. Penitentiaries and jails exist because whatever sin represents is a fact in society. Let us consider the Biblical teaching with respect to sin. The Hebrew of the Old Testament and the Greek of the New Testament each have not one word but several which are instructive as we define what is meant by this idea.

Eight different Hebrew words express this concept, each with its own particular flavor or definition of meaning. Of these, five have sufficient variety to warrant our attention. The first is *pesha'*, which represents the breaking of a known law, or deliberate rebellion against a rule or regulation that is laid down. We read that when Rehoboam succeeded Solomon, a delegation came to him to ask that the heavy yoke of service to the crown be lightened, a request that he refused. Thereupon Jeroboam led the northern tribes in revolt, and the passage concludes,

> So Israel has been in rebellion against the house of David to
> this day. (I Kings 12:19.)

The verb in this instance is *pesha'*; literally, "Israel sinned
against the house of David to this day." Sin that is rebellion is
deliberate. It is done consciously. This first word therefore represents transgression or rebellion.

A second word is *hattāth*, which properly means "error." It is
to make a mistake, to miss the mark, or to miss the road. We
read of the warriors of the tribe of Benjamin that

> Among all these were seven hundred picked men who were
> left-handed; every one could sling a stone at a hair, and
> not miss. (Judg. 20:16.)

The word "miss" is the word "to sin." One of the Proverbs
says:

> It is not good for a man to be without knowledge,
> and he who makes haste with his feet misses his way.
> (Prov. 19:2.)

The word for "misses his way" is the word for sin. The representation is of one hurrying along as the shadows of evening gather,
perhaps on a path that is not too distinct. As darkness falls, he
realizes that he is no longer on the path. He has missed his way.
He has sinned with his feet. To "turn aside," or "lose one's way,"
is the significance of this second word. The failure to arrive is
perhaps the besetting sin of most people today. It is not something they intended, not deliberate, but inadvertent. The goal
they have set for themselves is not reached. The target at which
they aimed is missed. This kind of sin truly describes the predicament of many of us. It is equivalent to error.

A third Hebrew word is *'āwôn*, commonly translated in the
English Bible as "iniquity." It represents something that does not
conform to a standard. A standard or norm has been set, but the
act does not conform. We might say that it is deformed, mis-
shapen, or awry. Perhaps the best English word for it is "wrong,"
for it applies to what is not right. Moreover, "wrong" is related
to the verb "wring," and what has been wrung is twisted, out
of shape. Many of us are subject to this kind of sin, for our lives

are twisted, out of shape, not in conformity with what they ought to be. Iniquity is therefore something that is not what it should have been. It is something that is not right.

A fourth word is *rāshā,* commonly translated "wickedness." This word is not often used in ordinary speech today, though it appears frequently in the Bible. It represents sin that has become a habit. It is applied to a form of action that has been repeated so often that it has become second nature. Transgression has been so frequent, error has been committed so many times, or wrong has been done so often that it has become a pattern. The modern phrase that is frequently used to describe such a situation is "the criminal mind," and this is precisely the concept of the Hebrew word. It indicates a person who has made the wrong choice so often that he may be counted on to do it again. His acts are predictable, because that is the kind of person he has become. The term indicates a reality that is perfectly comprehensible, for it is all too common. Personality is warped, and the Old Testament designates this habitual condition as wickedness.

A fifth Hebrew word is *'āshām,* usually translated "guilt." It represents a condition of blameworthiness, or a state of uncleanness. It is the result of any of the other words we have considered. We are all aware that guilt is a very real condition in our present day, and is not to be explained away by those who consider a doctrine of sin unpopular.

Three additional Hebrew words are used, but their meaning is substantially the same as the ones we have noted, for which they may be considered synonyms.

Turning now to the New Testament, we may take note of three Greek words that connote ideas similar to those we have examined. The first is *harmartia,* the commonest New Testament word for "sin." This is essentially equivalent to error, indicating that one has made a mistake, has done the wrong thing. Whether the mistake was deliberate or by accident is not the point at issue. The term simply indicates that one has erred.

A second word is *parabasis,* which denotes "to go alongside." The sense is that one has taken the wrong path, a divergent way instead of the correct route. It represents a turning aside.

A third word is *paraptōma,* properly meaning "to fall down alongside." The sinner is one who falls down by the way, or who falls aside. Thus we see that the three Greek words pick up elements that we saw in the Hebrew terms discussed.

The human failure, as represented in the words we have considered, is one of three kinds. It may be deliberate, intentional, or purposeful; or it may be due to carelessness, as when one misses the mark or falls by the way because proper precautions were not taken; or it may be due to what we may call simple human limitations. It is proverbial that " to err is human."

God's Response to Man's Sin

This is a comprehensive picture of what is meant when the Bible speaks of sin. How should God respond to this? Let us return to the illustration of the family. The child has been given freedom, makes the wrong choice, and does the wrong thing. What attitudes are possible so far as father or mother, brother or sister, may be concerned?

One attitude would be to blame him, to berate him, to condemn him, to punish him. He could be shut up in his room, put to bed without supper, or taken to the proverbial woodshed for a good spanking. The response is one of punishment, well deserved. The alienation warrants " getting back at him."

A second response would be to try to ignore what has happened. Parents would try to act as though the event had not occurred. No doubt some parents would prefer this kind of procedure to the punishment mentioned first. But responsible parents do not really act this way. The trouble is that this avoids the issue. To pretend that the mistake never occurred aids neither the child nor the rest of the family, and does nothing to prevent the mistake from being repeated. No growth would result from it. Simply to overlook the error is not enough.

A third response would be for the family to recognize what has happened, but to forgive the wrongdoer. They hold him responsible for what has taken place, but they do not hold it against him. They do not let it make any difference in their relationship.

They are willing to accept the event, but are ready to give him another chance, hoping that next time he will do the right thing. Opportunity is now available to correct what went amiss before.

These are exactly the ways in which the Bible represents God as responding to the errors and sins of men. Sometimes God is represented as angry and ready to punish human misdeeds. Again, God could be pictured as trying to overlook the sins of men, but actually the Bible seems to give little credence to this response, for if God is all-wise and all-knowing, it would be difficult to think of him as ignoring a fact, thus blinding himself to what has occurred. Rather, the characteristic Biblical response is that of forgiveness. The sinner is forgiven in order that a new start may be made. There is great emphasis, especially in The Psalms and in the New Testament, on the forgiveness of sin and on the new beginning that forgiveness makes possible. The Biblical teaching is that sin results in separation, but also that even though separation takes place, reconciliation is the divine purpose and goal.

Paul writes:

> Therefore, if any one is in Christ, he is a new creation; the old has passed away, behold, the new has come. All this is from God, who through Christ reconciled us to himself and gave us the ministry of reconciliation; that is, God was in Christ reconciling the world to himself, not counting their trespasses against them, and entrusting to us the message of reconciliation. So we are ambassadors for Christ, God making his appeal through us. We beseech you on behalf of Christ, be reconciled to God. (II Cor. 5:17-20.)

> For if while we were enemies we were reconciled to God by the death of his Son, much more, now that we are reconciled, shall we be saved by his life. (Rom. 5:10.)

The central fact in the doctrine of reconciliation is the work of Christ. To gain perspective, let us look at the ways in which the Old Testament represents God as forgiving. Again and again in The Psalms one comes across the fervent plea that God may forgive the sinner.

THE OLD TESTAMENT SACRIFICIAL SYSTEM

The first seven chapters of Leviticus contain a detailed description of the sacrificial system of the Old Testament. In all probability the ceremonies and rituals described are not something that prevailed in the wilderness, but are a reflection back into antiquity of the developed cultus of the Second Temple, that is, the elaborated worship procedures which came to prevail after the return from exile. It was set down in this third book of the Law, and reflected back as the teaching of Moses. We therefore see here the ways in which sin and atonement had come to be regarded.

Five different sacrifices are indicated for the forgiveness of sin. The first chapter describes the burnt offering. Here are the details showing how this offering is properly to be presented. Procedures are described if the offering is an animal from the herd or from the flock, or if it is a bird, a turtledove, or a pigeon. Details are given for what the priest does, how he burns certain parts on the altar, as "an offering by fire, a pleasing odor to the LORD" (vs. 9, 13, 17). As the smoke ascends to heaven, God receives it. This was the general practice among many peoples in ancient times and was believed to bring about the forgiveness of sin.

Chapter 2 describes the cereal offering, sometimes called the meal offering. This was the offering of agricultural products, for the Hebrews were not only herdsmen, but agriculturalists as well. Grain could be offered as such, or it could be baked into cakes or loaves of bread, leavened or unleavened, or flour could be offered. Oil was sprinkled or smeared on cakes or bread. This too was an offering made by fire, and the cereal offering also brought about the forgiveness of sin.

The third chapter describes the peace offering. Its characteristic feature was that the worshiper ate part of the offering, while the rest was burned on the altar. In theory, it really represented sitting at table with God, eating a meal together with deity, so that the worshiper was thought of as bound to deity by the covenant of salt, whereby an intimate relationship was thought to be established. The common meal brought the two together. The word "peace" in this instance is used in its basic Hebrew sense of "health." It does not connote international harmony, as it usually does today. *Shalom* in Hebrew is from a root that means "to be whole" or "to be complete." It properly signifies well-being. Jeremiah denounces the false prophets, saying,

> They have healed the wound of my people lightly,
> saying, "Peace, peace,"
> when there is no peace.
>
> (Jer. 6:14.)

To the ordinary English reader, this connotes some kind of international harmony. The prophet had nothing of the sort in mind. He is speaking of prophets who have no concern for national shortcomings; they say, "All is well, all is well," when all is not well. When a modern Israeli meets his neighbor, the greeting is "Shalom," meaning "health" or "well-being." The peace offering is therefore one that produces harmony, and a condition of well-being.

Chapter 4 describes what is designated as the sin offering. This is intended to obliterate the condition of guiltiness resulting from unwitting sins. An elaborate series of rituals is prescribed for the priest to perform. Parts of the animal are disposed of outside the camp, only the choice parts being burned on the altar. Part of the instructions concern the procedure if the whole congregation sins unwittingly, and concludes with the statement,

> Thus shall he do with the bull; as he did with the bull of the sin offering, so shall he do with this; and the priest shall make atonement for them, and they shall be forgiven. (Lev. 4:20.)

The phrase "the priest shall make atonement for him for his sin, and he shall be forgiven" recurs in vs. 26, 31, and 35, as well as in several instances in the succeeding chapter. It is clear that atonement is available through the proper ritual.

A fifth ceremonial is found in ch. 7. This is the ritual of the guilt offering. The Hebrew word for "guilt" means essentially "uncleanness." This offering is therefore designed to cleanse away the uncleanness resulting from transgression.

The custom of offering sacrifices is very ancient. The Hebrews inherited the practice from their neighbors. Sacrifices were offered in ancient Egypt, in Babylonia, as well as by the Canaanites, the Phoenicians, and other peoples of antiquity. The Israelites shared the institution with many others. Anthropologists are of the opinion that there are three possible origins of this rite. One is that sacrifice was originally a gift to deity to secure his favor or to avert his anger. It might be illustrated by the following situation. Consider the husband who is expected home for dinner at six o'clock in the evening. His wife has worked long and hard to prepare a delicious repast, but he is delayed at his office, and does not arrive until half past seven. What his wife has prepared is spoiled by the delay, and she feels a certain resentment toward him on this account. The feeling might be termed estrangement. So he stops on the way home to purchase a box of candy, or a bouquet of flowers, or an ornament of some kind, as a present for her. He understands that this will lessen what might have been a reason for estrangement. Of course, it could also be more than that; it could be a mark of his love and esteem for her. Perhaps the gift to deity might have this element also, but averting anger or securing favor is considered as one possible origin of sacrifice.

A second possible motive is the concept of sitting at table with deity. We have already commented on this, in connection with our discussion of the peace offering. To eat a common meal together was thought by the ancients to produce rapport and obligation which was significant.

A third suggestion is that sacrifice originated as an offering to secure the forgiveness of sin. Because the worshiper has done something wrong, he is under the obligation of making restitution. Sin has produced indebtedness, and the offering is payment for what is owed. Although many, if not most, would choose this as the probable origin of the custom, it is actually the least likely, because it presupposes a developed doctrine of sin. It is, no doubt, a later reinterpretation of the ancient rite. The actual origin must be one of the first two suggestions, and between them it is difficult to make a choice, since both of them might belong to the earliest of religious concepts.

BIBLICAL REPRESENTATIONS OF FORGIVENESS

Let us look at the Bible to determine exactly the Biblical concept of forgiveness. If we accidentally spill ink on a sheet of letter paper, our first act is to reach for a blotter to absorb what we can, and then to erase the stain as well as may be possible. Our purpose is to eradicate the discoloration. We must note immediately that nowhere in Scripture is forgiveness of sin represented as erasure of the act. Something that has been done cannot be undone. We cannot assume that what has happened did not happen. The deed is there. Not even God rubs out the fact of what has occurred. The past is always there. What the Bible does say is, for example, the following:

> Blessed is he whose transgression is forgiven,
>   whose sin is covered.
> Blessed is the man to whom the LORD imputes no iniquity,
>   and in whose spirit there is no deceit.
>
> (Ps. 32:1-2.)

The Hebrew word for "cover" is *kaphar,* which is also the verb "to make atonement." The metaphor is that the unsightly deed is covered over, or covered up, so that it is no longer visible. Everyone knows that it is there, but it cannot now be seen. Again, we read:

> Have mercy on me, O God, according to thy
>   steadfast love;
>   according to thy abundant mercy blot out
>   my transgressions.
>
> (Ps. 51:1.)

The figure here is not that of blotting paper soaking up ink, as some might suppose. Rather it represents, let us say, a view from a mountain peak that is blotted out by a cloud coming between the observer and the view. The cloud obscures the scene. The phrase "blot out" has this significance: something comes between the observer and the object that renders it invisible.

It is also linked with the figure of God averting his face from sin:

> Hide thy face from my sins,
>> and blot out all my iniquities.
>>> (Ps. 51:9.)

Here is the representation that God does not look upon wrong, but looks the other way.

Still another metaphor is that God does not remember or bring to mind the sin:

> I, I am He
>> who blots out your transgressions for my own sake,
>> and I will not remember your sins.
>>> (Isa. 43:25.)

> Be not exceedingly angry, O Lord,
>> and remember not iniquity for ever.
>>> (Isa. 64:9.)

> For I will forgive their iniquity, and I will remember their sin no more. (Jer. 31:34.)

The Biblical representations of forgiveness are therefore that God takes the initiative, by covering sin or by obscuring it, by hiding his face from it or by not bringing it to mind. We also find in the prayers of The Psalms the concept of cleansing:

> Wash me thoroughly from my iniquity,
>> and cleanse me from my sin!
>>> (Ps. 51:2.)

> Purge me with hyssop, and I shall be clean;
>> wash me, and I shall be whiter than snow.
>>> (Ps. 51:7.)

But in every instance, forgiveness is the result of the grace of God, not of the act of man. Forgiveness is not brought about by something that man does, but is due to divine mercy. Nowhere is it looked upon as something men deserve because they have earned it. The idea that a person could do penance which would make him worthy of forgiveness is foreign to Scripture. No amount of legalism is binding upon God. Forgiveness is a divine act on the part of a Creator who chooses not to take transgression into account. Therefore, we are not under law, but under grace. Forgiveness is possible, not because we have performed the correct rituals, but because it is the free gift of God.

The New Testament emphasizes the further teaching that the blood of Christ makes atonement for our sins. There come immediately to mind the words of John:

> For God so loved the world that he gave his only Son, that whoever believes in him should not perish but have eternal life. For God sent the Son into the world, not to condemn the world, but that the world might be saved through him. (John 3:16-17.)

To condemn the world would be to hold the world responsible, to blame men. But God wishes to save the world. He is ready to give the sinner a new start. Hence, he sent his Son for the purpose of saving.

Paul interprets this in Romans:

> For there is no distinction; since all have sinned and fall short of the glory of God, they are justified by his grace as a gift, through the redemption which is in Christ Jesus, whom God put forward as an expiation by his blood, to be received by faith. This was to show God's righteousness, because in his divine forbearance he had passed over former sins; it was to prove at the present time that he himself is righteous and that he justifies him who has faith in Jesus. (Rom. 3:22-26.)

The righteousness of God is demonstrated by the fact that he does not choose to regard or remember former sins. Moreover, he is willing to justify the person who has faith in Christ. This makes possible the new start of which we have spoken. Faith in Christ is the key to acceptance of forgiveness.

When John the Baptist, before he baptized Jesus, said: "Behold, the Lamb of God, who takes away the sin of the world!" (John 1:29) he did not mean that the sin would be erased. He meant that Jesus assumed his responsibility so that sin would not be man's burden. It is the testimony that God would not hold man responsible or to blame, but would be ready to offer forgiveness if man responded.

Paul writes:

> Indeed I count everything as loss because of the surpassing worth of knowing Christ Jesus my Lord. For his sake I have suffered the loss of all things, and count them as refuse, in order that I may gain Christ and be found in him, not having a righteousness of my own, based on law, but that which is through faith in Christ, the righteousness from God that depends on faith; that I may know him and the power of his resurrection, and may share his sufferings, becoming like him in his death, that if possible I may attain the resurrection from the dead. (Phil. 3:8-11.)

Paul understands that there is no righteousness of our own, based on law, or on having fulfilled the requirements for forgiveness, but that there is righteousness that results from faith in Christ that opens the way for the forgiveness of the Father. In the succeeding verses he asserts:

> Brethren, I do not consider that I have made it my own; but one thing I do, forgetting what lies behind and straining forward to what lies ahead, I press on toward the goal for the prize of the upward call of God in Christ Jesus. (Phil. 3:13-14.)

He indicates that he leaves the trappings of the past, which would hold him down, and presses on in the new faith, which centers, of course, in the redemption that comes through Christ. This is the doctrine of the atonement. It is the teaching that asserts the possibility of a new start.

The Meaning of Atonement

The English word "atonement" is derived from three elements: the words "at" and "one" and the suffix "ment." If a person is "at one" with someone else, he is *en rapport*. They understand each other and are in a harmonious relationship. If they are "at sixes and sevens," we understand that there is tension, conflict, and misunderstanding. When there have occurred acts and deeds that have brought about an estrangement between man and God, putting God and man "at sixes and sevens," the Biblical teaching is that through faith in Christ there can be reconciliation, putting an end to the tension and producing "at-one-ment."

We read in Hebrews:

> For it is impossible that the blood of bulls and goats should take away sins.
> Consequently, when Christ came into the world, he said,
> "Sacrifices and offerings thou hast not desired,
> but a body hast thou prepared for me;
> in burnt offerings and sin offerings thou hast taken no pleasure.
> Then I said, 'Lo, I have come to do thy will, O God,'
> as it is written of me in the roll of the book."
>
> (Heb. 10:4-7.)

What shall we say of the long years when priests followed the rituals of Leviticus, offering sacrifices to make atonement for sin? Are we to understand that they had no effect? When, in the days of Jeremiah, a worshiper sincerely followed the regulations, are we to understand that these were futile? I do not think so. I believe that the honest worshiper was truly forgiven when he followed the prescribed forms, because God has always looked on the human heart to discern its motives. True, the blood of bulls and goats does not undo the unrighteousness of sin, but the grace of God, evoked by the human response, is what brings forgiveness. God disregards the effects of sin if the heart of the sinner is repentant. If God sees a sincere and earnest worshiper in any generation, he will recognize him. The author of Hebrews is right when he declares that it is not the blood of bulls and goats that brings forgiveness. It is God's will, God's divine grace, that brings the longed-for result. Joel asserts:

> Return to the Lord, your God,
>   for he is gracious and merciful,
> slow to anger, and abounding in steadfast love,
>   and repents of evil.
>
> (Joel 2:13.)

This is the teaching of both the Old and the New Testament. The New Testament validates the Old Testament understanding of faith in the grace of God, and takes the position that this confidence is corroborated by faith in Christ.

Early Theories of Christ's Atonement

Through the centuries theologians have tried to reason how the work of Christ could have any effect upon you and me. Does the cross have validity for our times, and if so, how? A number of different theories of the atonement have been advocated at various times during the Christian era. It is of some interest that each of them has arisen through the dominant thought form of the period in which it was held. The earliest was the so-called " ransom theory," which arose in the period of the early church fathers. It was an age when the Roman Empire had established law and order, but in remoter parts of the Empire there was unrest, brigandage, and rebellion. Among the mountains were robbers who would go forth to plunder travelers and hold them for ransom; there was intertribal strife, the victors taking prisoners, and demanding ransom payments as the price of their release. In the fourth century, Ambrose, Bishop of Milan, spent all that he had, even melting sacramental vessels, to redeem captives after the Battle of Adrianople. Theologians noted such verses in The Letter to the Hebrews as:

For you had compassion on the prisoners. (Heb. 10:34.)

> Remember those who are in prison, as though in prison with
> them; and those who are ill-treated, since you also are in the
> body. (Heb. 13:3.)

Matthew notes the words of Jesus:

> The Son of man came not to be served but to serve, and to
> give his life as a ransom for many. (Matt. 20:28.)

Paul's word to Timothy employs the same metaphor:

> For there is one God, and there is one mediator between God
> and men, the man Christ Jesus, who gave himself as a ran-
> som for all. (I Tim. 2:5-6.)

Thus arose an interpretation of the atonement known as the
"ransom theory." Sin was conceived of as bondage; Christ was
the Redeemer, and his life was the ransom. Origen's position was
that the devil had enslaved man through sin, and God must buy
man back by paying Satan through the death of his Son. But the
devil miscalculated, for he could not keep the ransom payment.
Gregory of Nyssa (ca. 331–ca. 396) took a different view, namely,
that it was not Satan's self-deception, but rather that God prac-
ticed the deception. The transaction was a trick. The incarnation was a device to outwit the devil, and it succeeded. Later,
Gregory the Great pictured the flesh of Christ as bait on a hook
before Leviathan. As late as the twelfth century, Peter Lombard
pictured the cross as a "mousetrap baited with the blood of
Christ." The ransom theory was therefore also nicknamed the
mousetrap theory of the atonement. Its basic error was that it
made God subservient to Satan. There was a dualism that denied
the doctrine of the sovereignty of God.

The Middle Ages saw the rise of chivalry. The noble exploits
of knights and their ladies occupied a central place in the ideas
and literature of the times, and the several Crusades were undertaken to wrest the Holy Land from the infidels. An injury or an
insult to a person was regarded as a stain upon his honor which
could be remedied only by exacting satisfaction. Honor and satisfaction were keynoted in the thinking of the times. It therefore

seemed only natural that the atonement came thus to be interpreted. It was Anselm, Archbishop of Canterbury, who gave expression to what is known as the "satisfaction theory" of the
atonement. He reasoned that if man always rendered to God what
he owed, he would never sin. By paying what he owes, man honors God. By failing to do so, through sin, he dishonors God. But
God must not let his honor be thus defiled, since he is the moral
ruler of all. If he is to forgive, he must vindicate his authority either by punishment or by satisfaction.

This reasoning was in the mood of the age. It was the prevailing social attitude of the age of chivalry. If sin against God must
be atoned for, it must be either through punishment or through
satisfaction. Thus, only through satisfaction could punishment be
avoided. Anselm held that man himself was not in a position to
render satisfaction, since he already owed perfect obedience and
could do no more. He had no extra merit to make up for past sins.
Therefore, only through Christ could man be saved. Christ paid
for the sin and rendered satisfaction to restore honor to God. In
this theory, Christ was not punished for a sin he did not commit,
but gave satisfaction that the divine honor might be restored.
Moreover, Anselm held that the efficacy of the atonement was
not in Christ's death, but in his obedience and submission to the
will of God all through his life. This was what honored the Father. The cross was simply the climax of years of doing his Father's will.

POST-REFORMATION THEORIES OF THE ATONEMENT

In the two hundred years that followed the Reformation under
Martin Luther and his contemporaries, Protestant theologians
again addressed themselves to the question, among other issues,
of the atonement. Calvinists especially stressed the sovereignty of
God. God was conceived as an absolute monarch, and the keynote
of his rule was seen as legal. God was king, lawgiver, and judge.
Sin violated his laws, and sinners were criminals or traitors. To
forgive the sinner must violate the law of jurisprudence. Punishment was a divine necessity, and Christ offered himself as a sub-

stitute for the sinner. Hence this theory, formulated by the Synod of Dort in 1618, has been called the "substitutionary theory." Christ is still the ransom, as in the earliest church fathers, but the ransom is paid, not to Satan, but to God the King. It satisfies his justice. This is the theory that is enshrined in the Westminster Confession of Faith.

To this formulation it may correctly be objected that it makes a distinction between the Father and the Son that Scripture does not make. Scripture teaches that

> God was in Christ reconciling the world to himself. (II Cor. 5:19.)

The substitutionary theory distinguishes between God and Christ. God punishes, Christ suffers; God exacts the debt, Christ pays it. Moreover, to inflict punishment on one who is not guilty violates the very principle of jurisprudence to which the theory appeals. Calvin repudiated the contention that God's wrath was transferred from the sinner to his Son. Furthermore, the theory uses the Biblical term "reconciliation," but understands that Christ is represented as reconciling God to sinners, whereas Paul consistently affirms that the goal of Christ's work was to reconcile sinners to God (Rom. 5:10, II Cor. 5:18-20; Eph. 2:14-16; Col. 1:19-20). Biblical teaching is that enmity is all on man's side; God loves the sinner. Reconciliation is God's act, which he brings about through Christ. The substitionary theory in effect denies both these teachings.

The Dutch scholar Hugo Grotius (1583–1645) protested the substitutionary theory, and formulated what has been called the "governmental theory." His point was that God in the atonement acts, not as a judge or as a creditor, but as a ruler. His government is righteous, and a ruler may show clemency by relaxing or modifying the law's requirements. He does not simply pardon sinners, for this would merely confirm them in their ways. Furthermore, it would jeopardize, in man's sight, respect for the divine government of the world. Therefore God freely forgave man, but punished the sin. Christ suffered it, and by his noble example is a deterrent to man's further sin. The trouble with the governmental theory is that it saves the system at the expense of the individual. The governmental principle is more important than either Christ or man.

Finally, we should note what is called by many the "moral influence theory" of the atonement. The essence of this interpretation is that the death of Jesus on the cross was for the purpose of revealing the love of God in such a way that men are moved to repentance and to righteousness of life out of gratitude and loyalty. The effectiveness of the work of Christ is subjective rather than objective. It operates not because it satisfies a requirement, or fulfills a legal responsibility, but because it is a call to repentance and response. It changes the purposes and attitudes of those who observe it, and thus delivers them from both guilt and bondage. This view was put forth as early as the writings of Peter Abelard (A.D. 1079–1142), but was revived and given considerable support in the nineteenth century. Jesus is reported to have said, during the final week of his life:

> And I, when I am lifted up from the earth, will draw all men to myself. (John 12:32.)

If this is indeed an anticipation of the crucifixion, it would seem to be a support for this view. Further support may be seen in his word from the cross: "Father, forgive them; for they know not what they do" (Luke 23:34). Surely uncounted numbers of believers have been forgiven by the Father because they were forgiven by the Son. Such love does draw men to him.

The objection to this theory is that it is not really a characteristic New Testament idea, in spite of the quotations just given. Relatively few New Testament passages associate the love of God with the death of Christ. Among those which do we may note the following:

> "And as Moses lifted up the serpent in the wilderness, so must the Son of man be lifted up. . . ." For God so loved the world that he gave his only Son, that whoever believes in him should not perish but have eternal life. (John 3:14, 16.)

> But God shows his love for us in that while we were yet sin-
> ners Christ died for us. (Rom. 5:8.)

> By this we know love, that he laid down his life for us; and
> we ought to lay down our lives for the brethren. (I John
> 3:16.)

> In this the love of God was made manifest among us, that
> God sent his only Son into the world. . . . In this is love, not
> that we loved God but that he loved us and sent his Son to be
> the expiation for our sins. (I John 4:9-10.)

Theologians generally concede that although there is a truth here,
there is an objective as well as a subjective significance in the
death of Christ.

Perhaps a key to the way we should regard the atonement is to
think of God, not so much as judge, creditor, or ruler, but as Father. This is what Jesus continually emphasized. A true father
loves his child even though he errs. When a child strays, he is lost.
But the father's love and yearning is as strong as ever. Jesus said
he came to seek and save the lost (Luke 19:10). In the parable of
the prodigal son, Jesus taught the utter joy shown by his father
upon his return. Although he had squandered his property in
loose living, he was honored on his return, supplied with the best
robe, a ring on his hand, shoes on his feet, and a banquet to celebrate the fact that he had returned.

If we regard God primarily as Father, we realize that it may
not be necessary to think of him as demanding ransom, or exacting satisfaction, as a requirement for the restoration of an intimate
relationship with his children. These might be appropriate in a
judge, or a ruler, but hardly in a father. The fact is that in Christ,
our Elder Brother, God demonstrates his willingness to look the
other way, and not hold our faults against us. He is ever ready to
forgive; and in Christ's suffering on our behalf, he shows that it
is the nature of a father to undergo suffering for his child. Then
he indicates his readiness to entrust to us the message of reconciliation, to pass it on to others. This is the Christian gospel.

Theories of the atonement must remain theories. They are

man's attempt to rationalize a fact. But the ways of love are not always rational. There are interpersonal relationships that find their sources in other areas. True love is not something that can be categorized and explained. Emotions are hardly something that can be measured by a computer. Our relationship to our Creator is essentially a personal relationship based in some considerable measure on emotion as well as reason. The important thing is that we should recognize the fact of this relationship, rather than theorize about it. Divine forgiveness is perhaps beyond explanation, except on grounds of love and affection.

Let us further observe that the atonement is based on something that took place in history, but it has also a contemporary dimension. It still occurs, again and again, today. Whenever we are confronted by Christ and his challenge, by God and his forgiveness, our response opens the way for us to be atoned for today. Atonement is reconciliation, and reconciliation is contemporary as well as historic. It took place in the life and death and resurrection of our Lord, at a particular time in the past, yet it takes place repeatedly. It occurred in history, yet whenever men repent it occurs again. It is not only a finished act at a given point in past time. It is God's continuing way of dealing with his erring children.

VI · *Present and Future*

Many of us, if not most of us, are very much concerned with what we call "the good life." By this we mean living in ways that are pleasurable, happy, and carefree. We luxuriate in surroundings that are pleasant and easy. We take delight in the many modern inventions that have removed the drudgery of previous generations. Automobiles have cut to minutes travel that used to take hours. Automatic ovens cook dinners for us while we are away from home. Laborsaving devices in house and industry make tasks easy that used to be time-consuming and fatiguing. Automation is the magic word that is to deliver men from the burden of ceaseless work. Those who yearn for what were called "the good old days" are increasingly fewer. At least in the Western world, we live in an economy of abundance. In a large number of magazine articles in recent months, "the good life" is interpreted in terms of opportunities for self-advancement and leisure, of accomplishing necessary duties with less effort, and of having more time left for things we would like to do instead of things we have to do.

Yet we also look forward to days to come, trusting that the future will brings days even better than those we now know. Communication developments make it possible for us to know within minutes what is happening anywhere in the world. The jet travel age has so shrunk the globe that within hours we can be in places that used to take months to reach. Yet the human problem is still with us. We noted previously the parable of the Tower of Babel, typifying the difficulty that men have in getting along with one another. Men have not yet learned to live together in peace and harmony. Thus we yearn for days to come in which these problems may be resolved, as so many others have been, and when life will indeed be idyllic and utterly satisfactory for all. After all, what, exactly, is "the good life"?

The prevailing tendency is to define "the good life" in material terms. In this we may include advances of knowledge in the realm of health. Medical discoveries have eliminated many diseases, and new methods of prevention and cure make it unnecessary for us to fear ailments that brought terror to our grandparents. We may well anticipate that future discoveries will continue to eliminate disease and sickness, and certainly the expectancy of the span of human life has been tremendously increased in our time. Can we dare to hope that future advancement may be along other lines than material? We are in need of social renovation as well as material progress, spiritual welfare as well as physical well-being. In what terms would such welfare be conceived? Is there a goal toward which history is moving? What has the Bible to say about this question?

According to the New Testament, the goal toward which history moves is called the Kingdom of God. According to our earliest Gospel, Jesus began his ministry with the proclamation,

> The time is fulfilled, and the kingdom of God is at hand; repent, and believe in the gospel. (Mark 1:15.)

Matthew records:

> And he went about all Galilee, teaching in their synagogues and preaching the gospel of the kingdom and healing every disease and every infirmity among the people. (Matt. 4:23.)

Although the Gospel of John has very little to say about the coming of the Kingdom, there can be little doubt that it was central in the message of Jesus. It was his announcement as to the goal of the future. It was his proclamation of the age to come. Let us see whether we can determine more precisely what this conception involves.

THE IDEA OF THE KINGDOM OF GOD

The "Kingdom of God" means the kingly rule or dominion of the God who is believed to be the sole God of the universe. The idea is that of his sovereignty rather than of the place where that sovereignty is exercised. It is the rule of God over the hearts and wills of men, not a political or social entity. It is a kind of master purpose, or master plan, for the ordering of society according to the design of God.

Luke records the following:

> As they heard these things, he proceeded to tell a parable, because he was near to Jerusalem, and because they supposed that the kingdom of God was to appear immediately. He said therefore, "A nobleman went into a far country to receive kingly power and then return." (Luke 19:11-12.)

The word translated "kingly power" is actually the Greek word for "kingdom." The nobleman is not represented as going away to secure a realm over which to rule. He was not destined to rule over some far-distant country. The place of his rule was to be where he lived. The problem was that he was not a king. He was a nobleman. To exercise kingly authority he would need to secure the right to rule. The meaning of the word "kingdom" in this example is really that of "kingly power," and the Revised Standard Version has translated correctly.

An example of this situation is found in history in the period immediately preceding the advent of Christ. The Romans had taken over Palestine under Pompey in 63 B.C., but by the year 40 B.C. political conditions in Palestine had become very chaotic. Stability had been slow in coming. Herod the Great finally went to Rome, obtained the kingdom from the Roman Senate, and was declared king. Like the nobleman in the parable, he literally "went into a far country to receive a kingdom and then return." His kingly authority was to be king in Judea over the Jews. It is possible that Jesus had this particular situation in mind as he spoke the parable. But it shows that the Kingdom of God is not so much the place of his rule as it is his kingly authority or dominion.

Although the New Testament ascribes the idea to Jesus, he did not originate it. Its antecedents are very ancient. Though the phrase itself is infrequently used in the Old Testament, the idea that lies behind it is often expressed. As typical instances we may note the following:

> The Lord has established his throne in the heavens,
>   and his kingdom rules over all.
>
> (Ps. 103:19.)

> All thy works shall give thanks to thee, O LORD,
>   and all thy saints shall bless thee!
> They shall speak of the glory of thy kingdom,
>   and tell of thy power.
>
> (Ps. 145:10-11.)

> Thy kingdom is an everlasting kingdom,
>   and thy dominion endures throughout all generations.
>
> (Ps. 145:13.)

THE KINGDOM OF GOD IN THE OLD TESTAMENT

The beginning of the idea in the Old Testament was that the kingdom of Israel was the Kingdom of God. The Lord was conceived as the true King of the nation. Any earthly king was his representative. This is reflected in the accounts in First Samuel of the establishment of the kingdom. In the days of Samuel, the elders of Israel are said to have come to him with the demand, "Now appoint for us a king to govern us like all the nations" (I Sam. 8:5). Samuel prayed to the Lord, and the Lord said to him,

> Hearken to the voice of the people in all that they say to you; for they have not rejected you, but they have rejected me from being king over them. (I Sam. 8:7.)

Saul therefore was proclaimed king over Israel. He and his successors, David and Solomon, were solemnly anointed with oil as a token of induction into the office of kingship. They were considered to be "the LORD's anointed" (I Sam. 24:6; 26:11; II Sam. 1:14; 19:21; etc.). But this indicated that they had been chosen to rule on behalf of the Lord himself. The nation was looked upon as a theocracy. God was king; the ruling monarch was his representative. The kingdom was the Lord's.

David succeeded in unifying the nation and in gaining victory over the Philistines, which Saul was unsuccessful in bringing about. He had a spark of genius in him which made him the individual around whom the nation rallied. In spite of his personal shortcomings, later generations looked back upon him as the ideal king, sympathetic with the best ideals of Israel, the type and forerunner of the ideal king for which they came to hope. His kingdom was the Lord's, and the Kingdom of God was coterminous with the kingdom of Israel. They were the people whom God had chosen for himself (Deut. 7:6-8), not because they were more in number than any other people, but because the Lord loved them, and kept the oath that he swore to their fathers and by which he had redeemed them out of Egyptian bondage.

In the era of the great Old Testament prophets, the finger was again and again pointed to the fact that they did not deserve the appellation "Kingdom of God." The prophets judged the nation, calling attention to the sins and weaknesses of the people, summoning them to repentance and renovation. Punishment was announced for their national sins. Forgiveness and restoration were conditioned upon a change of heart and amendment of conduct. As we have previously noted, the Northern Kingdom fell to Assyria, and Judah to Babylon, and with the coming of exile, the prophets saw in this sequence of events the divine judgment on the nation. The house of David no longer ruled, nor did it ever return to sovereignty. The "Kingdom of God" had been brought to an end. The exiles in Babylon still formally acknowledged the Lord as their King, but the hope that the house of David would be restored became a wistful longing. Ezekiel pictures God as the Shepherd of his sheep, who will gather them out of the countries where they have been scattered, will bring them again into their own land, and restore David as their prince (Ezek. 34:11-24):

And they shall know that I, the LORD their God, am with them, and that they, the house of Israel, are my people, says the Lord GOD. (Ezek. 34:30.)

With the fall of Babylon, the people were at liberty to return to their homeland, in accordance with the prophetic hope. Many of them did return, but others of their compatriots preferred to remain in Babylon, where they had established themselves. Palestine was ruled successively by Persia, Greece, and the Hellenistic kingdoms of Egypt and Syria until the Romans took it over. The "Kingdom of God," as identifiable with Israel, never was restored. It remained an Old Testament hope. It is therefore understandable that, after centuries of frustration of this hope, the later Old Testament books began to look for a judgment upon the Gentiles, and thought of the Kingdom of God as breaking through the existing world order, to be established in an apocalyptic or eschatological sense. These are the themes in such passages as Zech., chs. 12 to 14, and The Book of Daniel.

So long as God's people suffered under the heel of heathen powers, the actual rule of God was incomplete. A concept of dualism began to arise in Jewish thought. They came to believe that there were fallen angels as well as sinful men. Demonic personages peopled the world in great numbers. They began to think in terms of a kingdom of evil that stood in the way of a coming of the Kingdom of God. Nevertheless, they did not give up longing for divine triumph over these demonic forces, and hoped against hope for the anticipated consummation.

This future consummation of the reign of God was closely connected with the Jewish "messianic expectation." But this hope, in the two centuries before Christ, was not so much primarily the coming of an Anointed One or Messiah, as it was the reestablishment of God's ancient rule over his people. The Book of Daniel (about 168 B.C.) envisages a resurrection from the dead for those who had remained faithful under persecution (Dan. 12:2-3). The opportunity to participate in the restored kingdom would therefore be available to numbers who were not part of the generation living when the restoration should take place. Earlier prophets did not have this expectation. But in the two centuries before Christ, there were various representations of God's otherworldly rule. Some of the apocalyptic writings express hope of a heavenly Jerusalem, of a new paradise, of a transformed earth, or other forms of salvation and consummation.

The Old Testament therefore looks forward to the Kingdom of God as an apocalyptic hope. It is characteristically referred to as " days that are coming " (e.g., Jer. 23:5; 31:27; Amos 9:13), or " in that day " (e.g., Hos. 2:16; Joel 3:18; Amos 9:11; Zech. 14:9). It is in contrast to this that the New Testament proclaims that the days are here. Jesus announced that the Kingdom was " at hand " (Mark 1:15), and that some who stood by would not taste death before they saw the coming of the Kingdom of God with power (Mark 9:1).

Several different terms are used in the Gospels as designation of the concept. Sometimes it is called " the kingdom of God," but it is also referred to as " the kingdom of the Father " (Matt. 13:43; Luke 12:32). Matthew does not use the phrase "kingdom of God," but refers to " the kingdom of heaven," evidently in order to avoid using the divine name, out of reverence or piety. It is the " kingdom of the Son of man " in Matt. 13:41 and 16:28; while in Luke 23:42 it is the kingly power of Jesus himself. Frequently it is simply " the kingdom," without additional designation (Matt. 4:23; 9:35; 13:19; 24:14; etc.). These terms all indicate the same idea. Dr. C. I. Scofield, in the annotated Bible that bears his name, attempts to make a distinction by assuming that one term designates the kingdom on earth, and another the Kingdom that is otherworldly. But this proposed distinction is unwarranted. It is disproven by the fact that in the parables of the Kingdom, appearing in the different Gospels, the terms are interchangeable in the same representations.

FOUR WAYS IN WHICH JESUS REPRESENTED THE KINGDOM

In the teaching of Jesus, the Kingdom is represented under four different types of symbolism. First of all, it is spoken of as though it were a *place* that could be entered.

> Not every one who says to me, " Lord, Lord," shall enter the kingdom of heaven, but he who does the will of my Father who is in heaven. (Matt. 7:21.)

Unless you turn and become like children, you will never enter the kingdom of heaven. (Matt. 18:3; cf. Mark 10:15.)

How hard it is for those who have riches to enter the kingdom of God! For it is easier for a camel to go through the eye of a needle than for a rich man to enter the kingdom of God. (Luke 18:24-25.)

But woe to you, scribes and Pharisees, hypocrites! because you shut the kingdom of heaven against men; for you neither enter yourselves, nor allow those who would enter to go in. (Matt. 23:13.)

It is better to enter the Kingdom with one eye than, having two, to be cast out (Mark 9:47). Men are said to be " near " or " far " from the Kingdom (Mark 12:34). It requires effort to enter (Matt. 11:12; Luke 9:62). After entrance has been secured, it is a place where even Jesus himself is pictured as eating and drinking (Matt. 26:29; Mark 14:25; Luke 22:16, 18). The representation of the Kingdom as a *place* is thus clearly evident.

A second class of passages represents the Kingdom as a *possession*. It is pictured as something that can be acquired. It is said of the poor in spirit and of those who are persecuted for righteousness' sake that " theirs is the kingdom of heaven " (Matt. 5:3, 10).

It is something that can be given or taken away. It can be taken away from the elders of the people, and " given to a nation producing the fruits of it " (Matt. 21:43). It is promised to " the little flock " (Luke 12:32). The parables of the treasure hidden in the field (Matt. 13:44) and the merchant in search of costly pearls (Matt. 13:45-46) give this view of it. As a most valuable possession, it is the peak of prosperity to secure it (Matt. 6:33; Luke 12:31).

A third class of passages represents the Kingdom as an *organization,* constituted of a certain class of men. It is a body politic, growing from small beginnings into something of large proportions and power. It is like a grain of mustard seed, which, when sown, grows into a great shrub (Matt. 13:31-32; Mark 4:26-27), or like leaven hid in three measures of meal, which increased until the entire lump was leavened (Matt. 13:33). Its members are the " sons of the kingdom " (Matt. 13:38). It is assumed that there will be leaders and officers, some kind of organization, but unlike civil officers, they are to be chosen because of their dedication to serve rather than for personal or prestige reasons. The mother of James and John, the sons of Zebedee, approached Jesus with the request,

> " Command that these two sons of mine may sit, one at your right hand and one at your left, in your kingdom." But Jesus answered, " You do not know what you are asking." (Matt. 20:21-22.)

He continued by indicating that the rulers of the Gentiles lord it over their fellows, and exercise authority over them, but that in his Kingdom " whoever would be great among you must be your servant, and whoever would be first among you must be your slave " (Matt. 20:25-27).

A fourth way in which Jesus represented the Kingdom was by designating it as *an order of things,* or dispensation. In the vision of the four beasts in Dan., ch. 7, there appeared " one like a son of man," who was presented before the Ancient of Days:

> And to him was given dominion
>   and glory and kingdom,
> that all peoples, nations, and languages
>   should serve him;
> his dominion is an everlasting dominion,
>   which shall not pass away,
> and his kingdom one
>   that shall not be destroyed.
>
> > (Dan. 7:14.)

The recipients of the Kingdom are further identified as " the saints of the Most High " (Dan. 7:25, 27), whose reward for steadfastness is a new and revolutionary order of things. The nearness of this order was what John the Baptist preached (Matt. 3:2). Jesus also proclaimed the coming of the new order; he sent forth his disciples to make the same announcement (Luke 9:2,

11), and in the Lord's Prayer he taught his followers to pray for its coming:

> Thy kingdom come,
> Thy will be done,
> Thy will be done
>   On earth as it is in heaven.
> Give us this day our daily bread;
> And forgive us our debts,
>   As we also have forgiven our debtors;
> And lead us not into temptation,
>   But deliver us from evil.
>
> (Matt. 6:10-13.)

The new order is spiritual in nature; its laws are essentially ethical. Humility and purity will make him who is least in the Kingdom of Heaven greater than John the Baptist, than whom no greater had yet arisen (Matt. 11:11; Luke 7:28). There will be no place for the self-righteousness and outward conformity of the chief priests and elders, of the scribes and Pharisees, for the Kingdom is taken from them and given to a nation producing the fruits of it (Matt. 21:43).

Since the parables given by Jesus as illustrations represent the Kingdom respectively under the forms of a *place*, a *possession*, an *organization*, and a *condition* or dispensation, we evidently are to understand that each of these figures in some way describes it. The composite picture is what we must keep in mind. Only so can it be comprehended adequately.

IS THE KINGDOM PRESENT OR FUTURE?

There is another seeming contradiction in the teaching of Jesus with reference to the new order. On the one hand it seems to be described as a future dispensation, breaking through into this world in apocalyptic fashion. Contrariwise, it is also described as a presently existing condition, evolving and growing here and now.

For more than half a century this apparent problem has occupied the attention of New Testament scholars. Several solutions have been set forth, but none of them seems wholly satisfactory. One view, advocated at the close of the nineteenth century, is that Jesus was in reality basically sympathetic to the apocalyptists, and looked for the coming of the Kingdom as an outward event to be ushered in with a display of supernatural power. This view would question the genuineness of sayings attributed to Jesus that represent the Kingdom as a present, evolving, and growing organism. It has been held that the ethical aspects of a present system are actually developments of a later date, the result of the work of the apostles, who came to see in their Master the fulfillment of the ancient hope, and who represented it, therefore, as part of his own message.

In contrast to this view is the opposite one, that the teaching of Jesus was essentially ethical, that he conceived the Kingdom as a present reality, and that the cataclysmic representations are due to his hearers who were unable fully to appreciate his purely ethical teaching, who thought in terms of the older apocalyptic ideas, and who included these as elements in the reported teachings of Jesus.

Again, it has been suggested that although Jesus conceived of the Kingdom in nonapocalyptic forms, he employed the apocalyptic usage because his hearers would be familiar with it. He accommodated the form of his teaching in such a manner as to make it intelligible to those who would not be able to grasp it otherwise. A variation of this view holds that he primarily understood the Kingdom to be a present and growing reality, but because this implies that it will some day be brought to complete consummation, this final triumph could legitimately be expressed in terms of its sudden realization according to the familiar pattern known to his contemporaries.

Still further to be noted is the view that has been called " realized eschatology." It is that the future coming of the Kingdom has actually taken place in the life, work, and teaching of our Lord. The future has become present. That which is to be has already become reality in him.

Then turning to the disciples he said privately, "Blessed are the eyes which see what you see! For I tell you that many prophets and kings desired to see what you see, and did not see it, and to hear what you hear, and did not hear it." (Luke 10:23-24.)

But if it is by the finger of God that I cast out demons, then the kingdom of God has come upon you. (Luke 11:20.)

From the ministry of Jesus onward, men have been living in the new age, in which the Kingdom of God, his grace and judgment, stand decisively revealed.

Each of these views, held separately, is inadequate. Each of them does violence to critical and exegetical methods. A certain arbitrariness is invoked in espousing any one. Perhaps the best we can do is to say that the Gospel record contains both representations — that of a process and that of a completed fact — and that there must be elements of truth in each. This kind of approach would be more faithful to the total Biblical record, and it may not be illogical, after all. There is a sense in which the Kingdom is here and now, and a sense in which it belongs to days to come. It may be both now and then. It may be here and yonder. It may be present and future.

Perhaps this could be illustrated from an incident in the history of World War II. From the perspective of twenty-five years, it appears that the decisive event in the defeat of Japan by the United States was the Battle of Midway Island. Previous to this, the American forces had been subjected to a devastating series of defeats. Beginning with Pearl Harbor, there had been successive setbacks, at Corregidor, the loss of the Philippines, of Guam, and of other strategic locations. Then, in the spring of 1942, the Japanese fleet made an all-out effort to take Midway Island. American ships and equipment were unequal to the Japanese. But with a combination of strategic moves, a decisive victory was gained by the United States that meant a complete reversal of the future complexion of the war in the Pacific. The Battle of Midway was the turning point. After this, there could be no doubt as to the final outcome. Japanese acknowledgment of defeat, and actual surrender, did not come until more than three years later. When shall we say that the war in the Pacific was won? Was it in 1945, when surrender acknowledged it? Or was it in 1942, when Midway assured the outcome?

Perhaps this may shed some light on how we regard the life and mission of Jesus. When does the Kingdom of God come? Is it when it is finally acknowledged by the surrender of the power of evil? Or does it come when the decisive stroke that signifies victory of divine authority over the powers of darkness is manifest? Both are represented in the New Testament record. Perhaps both should be retained, each without impairment of the other.

Jesus taught that the time was fulfilled. The Kingdom of God was approaching. It had already made itself known and was perceptibly close. At certain points it had already revealed itself as present. This breakthrough at particular points makes it clear to one who has rightly understood what is happening that the coming of the Kingdom in glory cannot be long delayed. What takes place during the present time while Jesus is actively at work leads onward toward complete fulfillment with the Last Judgment and the glory of the heavenly Kingdom. The remarkable thing about the teaching of Jesus in this regard is that he preached the purely eschatological Kingdom, which is to come with the final consummation of human history at some future date, as being already present here and now.

THE PRESENT AGE AND THE AGE TO COME

Only in recent years have scholars begun to appreciate another aspect of the concept of time in the Bible. It is now seen that the Biblical world view involves a linear concept, and that " eternity " as it belongs to redemptive history is simply unending time. Two different Greek words used in the New Testament are translated by the English word " world," but they have very different connotations. This is not apparent in the English versions of the Bible. There is, first of all, the Greek word *kosmos*. This indicates something which is in proper order or harmony, something which enjoys proper arrangement. Our word " cosmetics " is derived from this word. Cosmetics are preparations devised to arrange one's appearance properly. Their use assists us in making our appearance orderly. *Kosmos* indicates the sum total of all that constitutes an orderly universe.

But there is another Greek term frequently translated " world " which is often mistranslated in the King James Version. This word is *aiōn,* from which we derive our English word " aeon." It does not designate order or structure but, rather, a period of time. It may best be represented by the English word " age." If we trace the use of this term in the New Testament, we discover that there are two ages discerned, which are sometimes called " this age " and " the age to come." Note this usage in Matt. 12:32:

> And whoever says a word against the Son of man will be forgiven; but whoever speaks against the Holy Spirit will not be forgiven, either in this age or in the age to come.

Jesus is not speaking of two worlds, but of two ages. Man's total existence is conceived of as both in this age and in the age that is to come.

Paul speaks, in Eph. 1:21, of the exaltation of Christ

> far above all rule and authority and power and dominion, and above every name that is named, not only in this age but also in that which is to come.

The King James Version, by translating *aiōn* " world," produced a misconception. Paul is not indicating two worlds, but two ages. His term is not *ḳosmos* but *aiōn.* Two periods of time are envisioned, not two orders of society.

Mark 10:29-30 records that Jesus said:

> Truly, I say to you, there is no one who has left house or brothers or sisters or mother or father or children or lands, for my sake and for the gospel, who will not receive a hundredfold now in this time, houses and brothers and sisters and mothers and children and lands, with persecutions, and in the age to come eternal life.

In the first half of this verse, the term used is *kairos,* and in the second half it is *aiōn.* This makes it most clear that the reference is not to two worlds, but to two periods of time. In this time, in this age, we are to expect opposition and hostility to the gospel. In the age to come, those who have forsaken all to follow their Lord will be delivered from oppression and suffering, and will inherit eternal life.

The present age and the age to come are separated, in New Testament teaching, by the effective return of Christ and by the resurrection from the dead. It is said that as he sat on the Mount of Olives,

> the disciples came to him privately, saying, " Tell us, when will this be, and what will be the sign of your coming and of the close of the age? " (Matt. 24:3.)

This is not a question concerning the end of the world, but an iniquiry as to the beginning of the age to come.

The words of Jesus are again recorded:

> The sons of this age marry and are given in marriage; but those who are accounted worthy to attain to that age and to the resurrection from the dead neither marry nor are given in marriage, for they cannot die any more, because they are equal to angels and are sons of God, being sons of the resurrection. (Luke 20:34-36.)

This seems to say that in this time, in this age, it is incumbent to marry, rear children, and propagate the race; but in the age to come, different circumstances will prevail, and those who participate in that age will do so by way of resurrection.

The characteristics of these two ages, the present age and the age to come, are in contrast to each other. The present age is shown to be one in which evil, wickedness, and rebellion against God are prevalent. Galatians 1:4 indicates that Christ

> gave himself for our sins to deliver us from the present evil age, according to the will of our God and Father.

This age is characterized by sin and unrighteousness. It is an age from which men need deliverance, and this deliverance has been accomplished by the work of Christ.

In contrast to the present age we are presented with anticipation of the age to come. It is the age in which the evils of the present time are done away with, and in which the reign of the Father will truly be manifest. It is the age for which men hope and for which they pray. It is the age in which God's purpose comes into its own. It is the age of the Kingdom of God.

The blending of these two elements appears to be continued in the teaching of the apostles and in the rest of the New Testament. There seems to be no indication that one approach in any way excludes the other. In the letters of Peter, the apocalyptic view prevails, looking forward to the day when Christ's glory is revealed (I Peter 1:7 f.; 4:13). In The Letter of James, the inheritance of the Kingdom is something that will be the privilege of those who love their Lord (James 2:5). But in the book of Revelation, the Kingdom has come:

> And I heard a loud voice in heaven, saying, "Now the salvation and the power and the kingdom of our God and the authority of his Christ have come, for the accuser of our brethren has been thrown down, who accuses them day and night before our God." (Rev. 12:10.)

Those who are believers are already in the Kingdom and are rulers within it:

> To him who loves us and has freed us from our sins by his blood and made us a kingdom, priests to his God and Father, to him be glory and dominion for ever and ever. (Rev. 1:5-6.)

The seven churches are in the domain of Christ.

In the writings of Paul, both present and future are clearly apparent. Paul distinguishes two advents of Christ: the first coming in his incarnation has already resulted in the establishment of a community in which his disciples are fellow citizens with the saints and members of the household of God (Eph. 2:19), an era of the fullness of time, to unite all things in him (Eph. 1:10), the body of Christ (Eph. 1:23; 4:12; etc.), in which righteousness and peace and joy predominate (Rom. 14:17; cf. I Cor. 4:20). He transfers us to this Kingdom through faith in his deliverance (Col. 1:13). Yet this Kingdom in which believers now find themselves is also referred to as the one that will come " by his appearing and his kingdom " (II Tim. 4:1), and is to be inherited (Gal. 5:21). The Kingdom of Christ is said to be the means of furthering the Kingdom of God, for

> then comes the end, when he delivers the kingdom to God the Father after destroying every rule and every authority and power. For he must reign until he has put all his enemies under his feet. The last enemy to be destroyed is death. "For God has put all things in subjection under his feet." (I Cor. 15:24-27.)

The day in which we live is certainly in dire need of this double truth concerning the Kingdom of God. We do long for a future in which equality and justice may prevail, and we also are in need of saving help in our own time. The burning problems of our day are those concerned with racial and economic discrimination, with poverty and want, with inadequate housing and employment opportunities, with international tensions, with the elimination of war as an instrument of coercion, with overpopulation and its consequent results in food shortages, malnutrition, and famine, and with the further elimination of disease and illness. There are questions as to the use of the leisure time that has resulted from advances in technology, and the development of interests and occupations for older people, now retired, but who have a prospect of years of productive effort ahead. All of them are challenges to which the presence of God's grace in our time may bring constructive answers. It is not enough to look forward to some future day in which these problems will no longer exist. The remedial influence of Christian truth can and must be brought to bear in our time. This is the growing aspect of the divine Kingdom, and it is most appropriate and practical to the daily life we must lead.

If we are to think of the Kingdom as " at hand," as our Lord described it, we might think of it spatially rather than temporally. The average person learns to swim in an artificial pool. One end is shallow, the other is deep. There is a gradual slope so that the depth of water is perhaps between three feet at one end and eight to ten feet at the other. The novice steps into the shallow water and feels no fear. He can stand on the bottom with perfect confidence. Then, according to instruction, he may test to see whether he can float without touching bottom. He need not fear, for support is immediately available should he need it. Gradually confidence grows, and he learns that he can indeed float without having to rely on reaching out for solid support. He learns to move his arms and legs appropriately, and begins to swim. He then can move to deeper levels of the pool. He can still touch bottom, if need be, but eventually he moves out over his depth, confident that swimming at a depth of seven or eight feet is no different from swimming at three. But he is cautious. He swims along the side of the pool, not out in the center. He swims within reaching distance of the handrail at the edge. If there should be any faltering, any trouble, he could reach for the handrail. It would be his security. It would be at hand, should he need it.

Could we think of the Kingdom of God as " at hand " in this sense? Could it be that we should stress not so much its future coming as its present availability? Might it be that it is " at hand " if we choose to reach out and grasp it? If it is here and now, as well as then, why not make it fully available for the problems of our own day? Surely our Lord has given us the pattern of what it means. It remains only for men to bring it to reality by trusting it and living in accordance with its standards. It is fully available here and now. It belongs to the present as well as the future.

THE CHURCH AS THE KINGDOM OF GOD

It was only after the Christian church became a fully organized institution and began to influence the course of world history that a tendency arose to identify it with the Kingdom of God. This was first done significantly by Augustine. He most prominently identified the church as the New Israel, and saw it as inheriting the promises of the past, including the promises of the Kingdom. Whereas in Old Testament times there had been an identification of the Kingdom with the chosen people of Israel, Augustine envisaged the church as the now chosen people whom God had gathered to himself and made his Kingdom. This was the view that prevailed for several centuries.

In the days of the Reformation, men became conscious of the limitations of the organized church. They saw prelates and bishops seeking their own ends for personal advancement and achievement. For these self-seekers, the cause was not the goal, but their own positions and prerogatives. The Reformers considered this non-Biblical and non-Scriptural. Therefore they rejected the Augustinian view of the church as the Kingdom, and substituted the concept of the church invisible as the Kingdom. By the church invisible they meant to indicate that only God knows who are members of the true church. The elect are not those who formally constitute its membership, but all those who, through the centuries, have truly accepted the Lordship of Christ, and have responded in obedience to him. The church invisible consists of the number of persons, known only to God, who in sincerity and truth have acknowledged Christ's sovereignty. These are the ones through whom he has worked and will work; these are the elect, faithful, and true, through whom the will of God can be brought into its own. These are the sons of the Kingdom, and they comprise the Kingdom of God.

It is commonly said that we ought to be about the building of the Kingdom of God. Not infrequently we hear it said that this should be our purpose. Many a prayer has been spoken, asking that we be strengthened to build the Kingdom. This kind of reference is non-Scriptural. Nowhere in the Bible is there any reference to our building of the Kingdom. It is not our Kingdom, but God's. He builds it; we do not. Man-made kingdoms are utopias, and all utopias have been doomed to failure. The Christian faith is that man cannot work out his salvation apart from God. The Kingdom that must come is not of human making. It is of divine ordination, and unless it is so recognized it will fail. Human ordering of future prospects has always failed until now, and is doomed to future failure, unless it coincides with divine purposes.

Yet we can never take the attitude of the parody quoted by H. H. Rowley:

> Sit down, O men of God,
>   His kingdom let him bring,
> There is nothing you can do,
>   You cannot do a thing.

This would be a travesty on the whole teaching of the Kingdom of God. We are not to sit aside and wait. Though the Kingdom is God's, men must be active in their participation and expectation, in anticipation. There must be a conscious preparation for it, and a prayer that it may come. The Kingdom belongs to the future. But the future is the Lord's.

The hope for the days to come is both now and then. It is present and future. We look for the time when

> at the name of Jesus every knee should bow, in heaven and on earth and under the earth, and every tongue confess that Jesus Christ is Lord, to the glory of God the Father. (Phil. 2:10-11.)

Only then shall we find the fulfillment of the familiar prayer,

> Thy kingdom come,
> Thy will be done,
>   On earth as it is in heaven.
>   (Matt. 6:10.)

VII · *Christ and the Church*

The essence of Christianity today is the emphasis on Christ and the church. How shall the church be regarded as the instrument for realizing the Kingdom of God in our time? The church did not exist in the time of Jesus if we think of it as an organization. Of course, he chose the Twelve and sent them out to proclaim the coming of the Kingdom. Of one of them he said:

> And I tell you, you are Peter, and on this rock I will build my church, and the powers of death shall not prevail against it. I will give you the keys of the kingdom of heaven, and whatever you bind on earth shall be bound in heaven, and whatever you loose on earth shall be loosed in heaven. (Matt. 16:18-19.)

Jesus is not recorded as using the term "church" often. Though the later books of the New Testament use it repeatedly, in the four Gospels it appears only here and in Matt. 18:17. The Greek word represents the Hebrew word "congregation." It would seem that what Jesus had in mind was a renewal and renovation of the idea of the congregation of Israel, the people of God, united in acknowledging the sovereignty of the Most High, and dedicated to the fulfillment of his purposes in the world. The name "Peter" means "the rock," and his saying seems to indicate that upon this kind of person the solidity of the renewed congregation of Israel is to stand.

It was only after the experience of Pentecost, with the outpouring of the Spirit on his followers, that there came into being the entity we call the church, consisting of the followers of the risen Lord, who distinguished themselves from the more ancient congregation of God. As a consequence of Peter's impassioned preaching on that day, Luke records:

So those who received his word were baptized, and there were added that day about three thousand souls. And they devoted themselves to the apostles' teaching and fellowship, to the breaking of bread and the prayers. (Acts 2:41-42.)

These four elements were evidently the earliest evidences of the Christian community. Let us note precisely what they were.

FOUR CHARACTERISTICS OF THE PRIMITIVE CHURCH

First is the teaching of the apostles. They were not learned men, but they had known Jesus and could testify about him. When the rulers, elders, scribes, and priests later

perceived that they were uneducated, common men, they wondered; and they recognized that they had been with Jesus. (Acts 4:13.)

The apostles were ready to relate, probably in the Temple, to all who would listen, what they knew about their Master. In later times this would come to be known as Christian doctrine. At this stage it was personal testimony as to what they had seen and heard. Through the years that followed, this would be a first characteristic of the church.

A second characteristic was fellowship. There was a sense of community. Those who comprised the church knew that they had a great deal in common. Theirs was a profound sense of unity, mixed with a sense of joy and gladness (Acts 2:46-47). Hence, they came together frequently, to share their common faith and hope.

Thirdly, there was breaking of bread together. This was a further aspect of the fellowship just noted, but the idea of a common meal as a bond of unity is very ancient. As they " partook of food " together (Acts 2:46), they reemphasized the fact that they belonged together. This meal is to be distinguished from " the daily distribution " mentioned in Acts 6:1, which was evidently undertaken for the relief of distress; and it is also different from the beginnings of the Lord's Supper. Rather, it was *agapē,* a

" feast of charity " or " love feast," seemingly referred to in I Cor. 11:20-22 and Jude 12. Paul refers to abuse of it, in selfish ways, but it was another way of expressing their unity as a group.

A fourth aspect of the church was in " the prayers," which we are probably to consider as the thanksgiving connected with the common meal. The fact that the definite article is used with the word " prayers " indicates that something distinctive was meant, not simply participation in the regular worship of temple or synagogue, which were the ordinary forms of devotion in which the first Christians also participated (Acts 2:46; 3:1; Luke 24:53). It may be that in these prayers we see the very beginning of distinctively Christian worship.

At this early stage of the church, there was no organization. The apostles were naturally and inevitably thought of as leaders, and it is interesting that Peter called attention to the fact that, since Judas had betrayed his Master and afterward had died, only eleven remained. The church deemed it necessary to select another who had witnessed the ministry of Jesus to take his place. Matthias was chosen to complete the number twelve, so that the church as the New Israel would correspond to the number of the tribes in ancient times. The first and primary emphasis was to select one who could personally bear witness to their Lord and Master.

It is crystal-clear that Jesus was the center of the new faith. When the books of the New Testament came to be written and were collected for the use of the church, it was of course necessary to give a title to the collection. The books inherited from Old Testament times were called " the Law, the Prophets, and the Writings." The title page of the Revised Standard Version of the New Testament reads as follows: " The New Covenant, Commonly Called The New Testament, Of Our Lord And Savior Jesus Christ." This is the commonly accepted designation of the various writings that tell of the life and work of Jesus, of the beginnings of the church, and of the Christian doctrines that developed as the church thought about the implications of what it meant to be a follower of the Lord. Let us see exactly what is involved in this designation, and what it actually means.

THE BIBLICAL IDEA OF COVENANT

The title page of the King James Version had simply "The New Testament of Our Lord and Saviour Jesus Christ." The word "testament" in current English usage primarily means a legacy or will left by a person at his death. Jerome used the Latin word *testamentum* to translate the Greek *diathēkē;* hence the use of " testament " to designate the Bible in English. The Greek word did have the primary meaning of " dispostion of property by will," but even in classic Greek it also had the meaning of a " convention " or " arrangement between two parties." For this reason, the Alexandrian translators of the Greek Septuagint, when they sought for a word that would render *berith,* the Hebrew word for " covenant," chose this term, using it in the rarer and secondary sense.

In its use in the Old Testament, a covenant was, broadly speaking, a compact or agreement between two persons or two groups of people. Abimelech at Gerar entered into a covenant with Abraham (Gen. 21:27), and afterward under similar conditions with Isaac (Gen. 26:28). Abraham entered into covenant with the Amorites (Gen. 14:13), Laban with Jacob (Gen. 31:44), Jonathan with David (I Sam. 18:3), Solomon with Hiram (I Kings 5:2-6), Ahab with Ben-hadad (I Kings 20:34), and numerous other instances could be cited. The word is used to designate a treaty between nations, as when Amos said of Tyre,

> For three transgressions of Tyre,
>   and for four, I will not revoke the punishment;
> because they delivered up a whole people to Edom,
>   and did not remember the covenant of brotherhood.
>
> (Amos 1:9.)

But in Biblical usage, this general conception developed into a much more specific one. Three additional elements may be noted. First, as a contract includes a binding element or creates an obligation, so a covenant becomes a bond, imposed by two covenanting parties on each other, or by one upon himself and the other. Thus Jehoiada the priest put the Carites and guards under covenant by oath to protect Joash, the young son of Ahaziah, who was to succeed to the throne of Israel (II Kings 11:4 ff.). A second additional element is that a covenant is not merely a contract between and before men. God is invoked in it as a third party. He is considered as having a share in its terms and its results. An oath, a curse, or a sacrifice is thought to be an indispensable ceremonial accompaniment of the agreement. A third aspect is that a new relation is regarded as coming into being between the two contracting parties. This could be symbolized by a common meal or by pouring out sacrificial blood as a libation, and this was seen as the sign of a new and irrevocable relationship, whose object was mutual benefit and advantage. The contracting parties were bound to regard each other as members of a new organic entity. The breaking of such a covenant is loathed and denounced by the prophets in no uncertain terms (e.g., Hos. 6:7; 8:1; 10:4; Isa. 24:5; Jer. 11:10).

Just as men entered into covenants with one another, so the Old Testament writers came to believe that God entered into such a relationship with men. He was said to have established this bond with Abraham (Gen. 15:18), and when the account of the confrontation of the people of Israel with God at Mt. Sinai came to be written, it was in terms of the entire nation entering into covenant with the Lord, who promised to be their God and they his people. The covenant at Mt. Sinai is a leading feature of the Old Testament story.

Because of the laxness and failure of the nation to live up to the responsibilities enjoined by such a relationship, the prophets despaired of its continuance. However, they continued to have faith that the rupture would not be final (e.g., Hos. 1:9 f.; 2:23; 3:3). The outstanding passage is, of course, in Jeremiah, where that prophet envisages a New Covenant, not like the Sinai covenant that was broken, but one that would have three distinguishing characteristics: (1) it would be inward rather than external, marked by spiritual features; (2) it would be universal, for although made with Israel and Judah, its benefits would extend to all men; and (3) it would be marked by the forgiveness of sin (Jer. 31:31-34).

The New Testament faith is that the gospel of Christ has brought this New Covenant to reality. The author of The Letter to the Hebrews makes this very explicit. He quotes the entire passage in Jeremiah (Heb. 8:8-12), and shows how the priestly work of our Lord is its fulfillment. When, therefore, we seek a title that will comprehensively describe what the books of the New Testament are all about, there could hardly be a better designation than "The New Covenant, Commonly Called The New Testament, Of Our Lord And Savior Jesus Christ."

THE TITLE PAGE OF THE NEW TESTAMENT

The name "Jesus" is the Greek equivalent of the Hebrew name "Joshua," which means "the Lord is salvation." Matthew records the announcement of the angel to Joseph:

> You shall call his name Jesus, for he will save his people from their sins. (Matt. 1:21.)

His name is thus appropriate to what the church sees in his life and work. "His people" is the honorary title of Israel. The salvation referred to is probably conceived in that half-spiritual, half-national fashion which is so vividly described in the poetic prophecy of Zechariah found in Luke 1:68-79. Some of the elements of the salvation and redemption of "his people" as there depicted are that "we should be saved from our enemies, and from the hand of all who hate us" and "that we, being delivered from the hand of our enemies, might serve him without fear, in holiness and righteousness before him all the days of our life." The knowledge of salvation is through the forgiveness of sins.

Throughout the ministry of Jesus, the word "to save" is for the most part used of miracles of healing, or deliverance from bodily danger, as in the instances of the woman healed of a hemorrhage (Matt. 9:21), the storm-tossed boat in danger of being swamped by heavy waves (Matt. 8:25), and Peter's attempt to walk on the water (Matt. 14:30). Since they were conditioned by faith, which involved a personal and spiritual relation to Jesus, blessings of a higher order were involved, and these are no doubt included in such expressions as "Your faith has saved you" (Matt. 9:22). When we read that "the Son of man came to seek and to save the lost" (Luke 19:10), it is the deeper spiritual sense that is involved, as is usually so also in the characteristic usage of the Fourth Gospel (e.g., John 3:17; 5:34; 10:9; 12:47). Here also Jesus is expressly characterized as "the Savior of the world" (John 4:42). It was his vocation to bring eternal life to all men.

But Jesus is also the Christ. The Greek word *christos* is the equivalent of the Hebrew word *mashîâh,* "the anointed one." This is, of course, the term used of the kings of Israel who were anointed with oil upon their induction into royal responsibilities. It also came to be the designation of the expected ideal king who should fulfill in the Messianic Age what the kings of Israel and Judah had failed to accomplish in history. Priests, as well as kings, and occasionally prophets, were anointed as a sign of their elevation to high functions.

The messianic idea should not be considered as limited by the meaning of the word "messiah." It includes all the aspirations of Israel toward worldwide influence from the very beginning. Long before a particular person was fixed upon to carry out God's plan of righteous rule on earth, there had been an expectation that the Lord would confer such a blessing on the posterity of Abraham that all nations would "bless themselves" in Abraham and his descendants, that is, ask such a blessing for themselves (Gen. 12:3), and that there would be a succession of prophets who would communicate God's will to Israel (Deut. 18:18). It is formally held that the earliest foreshadowing of such an aspiration is found in Gen. 3:15, where it is said that the "seed of the woman" should (eventually) "bruise" the head of the serpent. This is an expression of the hope that the ills afflicting humanity would eventually be healed, and that the adverse effects of the "fall" of man would someday be rectified.

It is in The Book of Isaiah that the concept of the coming of an ideal king first comes into its own. In a poetic passage it is portrayed that

> To us a child is born,
>   to us a son is given;
> and the government will be upon his shoulder,
>   and his name will be called
> " Wonderful Counselor, Mighty God,
>   Everlasting Father, Prince of Peace."
> Of the increase of his government and of peace
>   there will be no end,
> upon the throne of David, and over his kingdom,
>   to establish it, and to uphold it
> with justice and with righteousness
>   from this time forth and for evermore.
> The zeal of the LORD of hosts will do this.
>
> (Isa. 9:6-7.)

Further passages in Isaiah, in Micah, in Jeremiah, and other prophets enlarge upon this theme, and when the house of David had fallen, the hope of restoration flourished during the exile.

The message of the church came to be that in Jesus there is the fulfillment and realization of the messianic hope. Jesus is therefore proclaimed " the Christ." It is to be noted that this is a title, an office, not a name. Because in later books of the New Testament the combination " Jesus Christ " or " Christ Jesus " is so often used, we moderns are constrained to think of the term as a name rather than an office. We do well to think more precisely on this matter, and to realize that what we express in using the term " Christ " is really a function rather than a name.

There is one further word on the title page of the New Testament that remains to be considered. It is the " New Covenant of Our *Lord* and Savior Jesus Christ." For the essence of discipleship is the recognition of Jesus Christ as Lord. Allegiance to him and his cause is all-important. Responding to his Lordship is the key to Christian commitment. Unless Christ is Lord of all of life, we fall short in our response to him.

In English, the word " lord " has as part of its background the feudal system of the Middle Ages. In those times, the lord lived in a castle on a hill, and the villagers and common folk lived in a town below. They stood in the relation of fiefs to the lord. They were bound to him in allegiance, and he could call upon them for various services. If the fields needed tilling, he gave the order for the people to do it, and they obeyed. If there was danger of intrusion or invasion, he could call them to arms. They were his servants, so to speak. They were bound to obey his commands. Many a historian has deplored feudalism, deeming it unjust in many ways. Nevertheless, there is something to be said on the other side. The concept of the nation had not yet crystallized. There was no sense of national security. If banditry or invasion threatened, what could the poor man in the village do? He and his village would be at the mercy of the intruder. As a matter of self-protection it was in his best interest to bind himself to the lord in the castle, so that in time of danger the lord could take the initiative and see that whatever was necessary would be done. In time of stress, the villagers could be protected within the castle walls. The system provided a place of refuge in a day of insecurity. The system was based on allegiance of fief to lord.

This feudal relationship may illustrate in a partial way what we mean when we think of Christ as Lord. The same kind of loyalty that made ultimate mutual help and protection in the Middle Ages is what should characterize the relation of the Christian to his Master. He can respond to us only if we respond to him. The freedom of the life in Christ is possible only when utter commitment to him and his cause precedes. When we are bound to him we are truly set free. This is the Christian paradox. The recognition of superior authority, and acceptance of responsibilities implied by it, makes possible true Christian liberty.

It is said that Lord Nelson, commanding the British fleet, once brought about the defeat of the ships of France. The French Admiral came on board Nelson's ship in surrender. He was of course of equal naval rank with Nelson, and it is reported that he strode up to Nelson, proffering his outstretched hand in token of equality. Nelson did not extend his hand. Standing firmly erect, he said, " First, Sir, your sword! " There could be no recognition of equality until there had first been the token of submission.

Perhaps this illustrates further what is implied when we speak of Jesus Christ as Lord. He is willing to extend his hand to us if we are willing to make him Lord indeed. Unless we recognize his Lordship, we fall short of bringing the gospel to realization.

WHAT IS THE CHURCH?

Returning now to the subject of the church, made up of those who acknowledge Jesus Christ as Lord, we note that the English word "church" is the translation of the Greek word *ekklēsia*. The Greek is reflected in such a word as "ecclesiastical," meaning "churchly." It is composed of two elements, the preposition "out" and the verb "to call." The church is those who are called out. There have been those who have understood this to mean that the church is called out of the world, that it is separated from the world, that it must have nothing to do with the world. This is a false conclusion. God loved the world so much that he sent his Son to be its Redeemer. The church must be part of the world if it is to be the vehicle of God's saving grace. Rather, the word signifies that the church is called out so that it can be identified. Its members are called out, and, so to speak, they step forward and are seen together as a particular group with an identity of its own.

In the Greek translation of the Old Testament, *ekklēsia* is used to translate the Hebrew *kahal,* which we render as "congregation." The root meaning of this term is "to call together," or "to come together," "to assemble." As the congregation of old came together, it became identifiable. The theme in common between the Greek and Hebrew words is therefore a matter of identity. In later Jewish days there arose the synagogue, which also has the root meaning "to come together." The various words, therefore, all point to a group that finds unity because the members have something in common. In the case of the church, it is the gospel of our Lord and Savior Jesus Christ.

The Reformed understanding of Scripture is that a child is born into the church if he has parents who are part of the church. Not all Christian groups so believe. Baptists, for example, do not take the view that a child is born into the church; they hold that when he reaches years of discretion, he must then choose whether he will join the church or not. It is an act of decision on his part at the age of ten, or twelve, or fourteen, or whenever he is old enough to make his own choice and understand what he is doing. None of the churches that hold the Reformed faith take this position. Presbyterians believe that the church is the household of faith, and a child is born into that household. The formula of infant baptism asserts that the child is baptized in the name of the Father, Son, and Holy Spirit, and is now received as a member of Christ's church. His name is enrolled on the list of baptized members, and if his parents are dismissed to another congregation, the child's name is also included. His parents have chosen for him. They have taken upon themselves the obligation of guiding him in the Christian way until he arrives at the age where he can take the responsibility upon himself.

When he reaches the age of twelve to fourteen years, and is ready for the step, he takes his stand before the congregation to be admitted to the Lord's Supper, and to reaffirm his baptismal vows in his own right. He does not " join the church," for he is already a member. He assumes for himself the vows taken on his behalf some years earlier. This assumption by the Reformed Churches is basic to our conception of the church.

Not infrequently we learn of parents who assert that they do not want to choose a particular church for their children. They affirm that the child should make a free decision when the time comes. Why should they prejudice that choice? In answer to this point of view, let it be noted that when a child is born, he is born an American citizen if his parents are American. From the moment of his birth he is a citizen of the United States, entitled to all the protections and privileges of any citizen. He is registered at the county courthouse. The community recognizes him as one of its members. He will be entitled to education at public expense when he reaches the proper age. There is no question as to his acceptance as a citizen. Eventually he may be expected to come to the age of maturity, at which time he will be given the privilege of the ballot and will participate fully in the responsibilities as well as the privileges of citizenship. It would be utterly ridicu-

lous to take the position that a newborn child is without nation-
ality, and when he arrives at the age of discretion he will then be
allowed to choose whether he wishes to be Chinese or Chilean,
Nigerian or Italian. We consider it right and natural to be born
into the nation. Why should not a child also be born into the
church of Christ?

It is a tendency of society to identify its various members with
diverse groups with which they associate themselves. Many of us
are members of athletic associations or golf clubs, lodges or fra-
ternities, luncheon clubs or social organizations. We find satisfaction and achievement in working cooperatively in such groups.
The effectiveness of the individual is greatly increased by membership in a recognized society. So it is also with the church. The
individual Christian is not alone. He is one of a congregation. He
is part of an identifiable group. The united witness of all its
members is far more effective than the total witness of a number
of unaffiliated persons. The church is an entity of its own as well
as the sum total of those who comprise it.

THE CHURCH AND THE WORLD

Because of the task confronted by the church, certain principles are seen to emerge. What is the relation of the church to the
world? The author of The Letter of James says:

> Religion that is pure and undefiled before God and the Fa-
> ther is this: to visit orphans and widows in their affliction,
> and to keep oneself unstained from the world. (James 1:27.)

The First Letter of John states:

> Do not love the world or the things in the world. If any one
> loves the world, love for the Father is not in him. (I John
> 2:15.)

Yet the best-known verse of the New Testament states that

> God so loved the world that he gave his only Son, that who-
> ever believes in him should not perish but have eternal life.

For God sent the Son into the world, not to condemn the world, but that the world might be saved through him. (John 3:16-17.)

It is obvious that the word " world " is used in these passages in two different senses. In one sense, the world consists of all the people who make up society. This is the world that God loved, and to which he sent his Son to be its Redeemer. In the other usage, the world consists of the things that are worldly as opposed to spiritual, material as opposed to ethical, temporal as opposed to eternal. In this sense we are warned against accepting what is inferior instead of striving for what corresponds to the upward call of Christ.

It is not the teaching of the Bible that the church is to be separated from other people. The point to the passages just quoted is that members of the church should not become involved in concerns and interests that are below the level of what the Christian faith involves. They are, indeed, to be involved in the world, but in ways that serve the world, lead it upward toward higher goals, and aid in making it the kind of world that will conform to the ultimate goals which will realize the Kingdom of God.

THE ORGANIZATION OF THE CHURCH

We have already indicated that there is no New Testament pattern as to how the church should be organized. The apostles were the early leaders, for reasons we have given. Paul considered himself an apostle, called by Christ (e.g., Rom. 1:1; I Cor. 1:1; 9:1-2; etc.). As need for some kind of additional organization appeared, steps were taken to fill the need. Acts 6:1-6 relates the appointment of seven men of good repute, " full of the Spirit and of wisdom," whose responsibility it would be to administer to the needs of widows and others in the Christian community as this was warranted. There is no hint of an institution divinely ordained and fixed, now being put into effect. A new need emerges in the church's life, and practical steps are taken to meet it. It is irrelevant to ask whether the Seven were deacons; later on, to be a deacon was to have a particular office. These seven men were not invested with an office, but were chosen to perform a particular duty because there was a need for it. Stephen, who was later martyred, was one of them (Acts 7:58), as was Philip, who encountered the Ethiopian on the way to Gaza (Acts 8:26-40). The Seven were therefore capable of much more than ministration to the needs of widows. They were, indeed, " full of the Spirit and of wisdom."

Without warning we come across " elders " in Acts 11:30. They were no doubt older men of experience, whose advice and leadership were considered valuable. It was so natural that any Jewish society should rule itself by " elders " that the historian takes their existence for granted. They are linked with the apostles in Acts 15:2, 4, 6, 22, in such a way as to indicate that they had a significant part in the administration of the church in Jerusalem. The " whole church " (Acts 15:22) is associated with them, but the apostles and elders are depicted as guiding its deliberations and formulating and carrying into effect its decisions. They seem to have supervised the spread of Christianity and to have maintained in this way the sense of unity of the church.

Prophets are also mentioned, several by name (e.g., Acts 11:27; 13:1; 15:32); also, an inspired kind of " teachers " (Acts 13:1). Anyone might " speak the word " who had the spiritual gift to do so (Acts 8:4; 11:19). In point of fact, much of the diffusion of the gospel was due to these unofficial and unordained preachers.

Not infrequently we hear it said that we ought to return to the simplicity of the primitive church. It is asserted that the ecclesiastical organizations that have developed through the centuries have obscured the values of New Testament days. But the situation is different when Christians are numbered in hundreds of millions instead of in scores. The situation that prevailed when most Christians knew each other personally is quite other than the situation that prevails today. Therefore, various forms of more intricate organization have evolved through the years to meet new situations. Just as the primitive church devised methods of coping with the problems that confronted it, so later generations have created other forms and institutions to serve their needs.

We recognize today several branches of Christendom. We are part of the Western Church, which came into being as Latin Christianity. But there is also the Eastern Church, known generally as the Orthodox Churches — the Greek, Russian, Bulgarian, Slovakian — which have an ecclesiastical calendar different from that of the Western Churches. In Africa is found the Coptic tradition, which also is very ancient. The Armenian Church is another tradition. There are younger churches in India, Japan, and various African countries. Each has its own kind of organization. Whereas in the early church there was an absence of form of organization, today there is a multiplicity of forms. Any or all of these can represent the church.

The great peril is that the church may be confused by the forms in which it is conceived. The organization tends to be viewed as the entity itself. The perspective of church development indicates that this is a fallacy. Any form of organization is something devised to meet current needs. No particular organizational pattern is Scriptural. All are called forth and appropriate to the needs of the moment. Christianity is not primarily a form of organization — it is a way of life. It is what Jesus taught in the Sermon on the Mount and in the parables.

Through the years there have been great Christians whose expression of their faith and their understanding of the Christian gospel has varied in many ways. There have been great Christian theologians who have pondered the implications of Christ's redemptive activity; there have been mystics who have seen the faith as an intimate and personal experience of that redemption; there have been activists such as Francis Xavier, who organized his followers as an army to go out and take the world for Christ. Such different expressions of the consequences of faith in Christ, and loyalty to him, are evidence that Christianity is not a particular pattern, but a way of life and a recognition of the truth of Biblical religion.

Biblical teaching recognizes God not only as Creator and Sustainer of all things, but also as one who works in human history and whose acts are discernible in history. His requirements are ethical rather than formal or mechanical. In Christ the Lord our faith recognizes a revelation of God. Philip said to Jesus:

> " Lord, show us the Father, and we shall be satisfied." Jesus said to him, " Have I been with you so long, and yet you do not know me, Philip? He who has seen me has seen the Father; how can you say, ' Show us the Father '? Do you not believe that I am in the Father and the Father in me? The words that I say to you I do not speak on my own authority; but the Father who dwells in me does his works." (John 14:8-10.)

The God who is thus revealed is ever ready through suffering to bring about the redemption of men. Because God raised Christ from the dead, we dare to hope that he will one day do the same with us. The Bible does not teach immortality, but resurrection. God only is immortal; we are not. We are not taught that there is something in man that will not die. We are taught that it is divine initiative that can bring to life. If God could create once, he can create again. The meaning of the resurrection is related to the idea of the transformed life, one which is remade by the grace of God.

The view of Christ and the church that we have been considering leads to a new sense of mission regarding our own time. A century ago, and much more recently in some quarters, an attitude prevailed that the place of the church was apart from the world. In order to be religious, one should withdraw from society. This was, of course, the reasoning that brought the monastic movement into being. In order to be religious, men withdrew into monasteries, became monks, and devoted their entire time to meditation, prayer, reading, and joining in hymns and psalms. So, more recently, the church was conceived as an enclosure within four walls, where one could withdraw from the world to gain satisfaction in comparable acts of devotion. We now understand that the true church is not a building into which to withdraw, but is a way of living out in society. The mission of the church is to witness by word and act where other people are. The church must be concerned with race relations, civic service, war and peace, proper use of leisure time, and with bringing constructive criticism and commentary on the society in which it finds itself. Any church that becomes adjusted to its surroundings has lost the gospel. If a society is ungodly, we have no business to become adjusted to it. We ought instead to be so dissatisfied with it that we make every effort to remedy what is wrong. This means there must be consecrated churchmen and churchwomen in the affairs of daily life — in business, in corporations, in labor unions, in government — to make the gospel influential in all walks of life, in consistent witness to the things we believe and have in common. This is the church in the world, not the church withdrawn from the world.

EVIDENCES OF THE INFLUENCE OF THE CHURCH

In these days when doubt is so frequently expressed over the influence of the church, when it is said that the impact of Christianity is on the wane, it is heartening to observe that over the years the church has had more effect than many would acknowledge. There was a time when education was almost exclusively the prerogative of the church. The monasteries were centers of learning. They were almost without exception the places where education flourished. The church emphasized the need for an educated laity. Gradually the rest of society began to understand, and public education became the responsibility of government. It is now recognized as the responsibility of all the people.

The same is true of hospitals. There was a day when the sick were simply the unfortunate. No one was consistently concerned for them except the church. But because the church had compassion, society was compelled to admit that the care of those who are ill is the responsibility of the community. Now we have public hospitals and private hospitals, we have hospitals conducted by universities and foundations, and the coming of Medicare is a public service recognized as a responsibility of government. Except for certain mission locations, where the public does not yet recognize its duty, the church no longer finds it necessary to operate hospitals.

Similarly, the church led the way in making provision for the care of orphaned children and the care of the aged. No one else felt a sense of responsibility until the church showed, by its concern, that these were areas of human need. Now the church is gradually turning its orphanages to other uses, since society itself sees that here is a public duty; and cooperative homes for aging citizens, financed in various ways by community effort, make it unnecessary for the church to provide for them.

Until very recently, concern for the improvement of conditions in underdeveloped parts of the world was chiefly shown by the church. Missionaries with highly altruistic motives left their homes to serve in faraway lands where people needed help. They were sent out by the church. Now we have seen the rise of the Peace Corps, not under the church, but sending out young people with the same kind of dedication to the service of others that characterizes missionaries. In our own country VISTA is further proof of the rising tide of altruistic concern.

These are examples of the influence of the church in the world. In our day the church is now free to center its concern on new areas of need, and again to point the way in which society must move. Past experience should encourage us to have high hopes for the future. If the church can make its influence felt on such issues as war and peace, opportunities for minorty groups, elimination of racial prejudice, fair practices in employment, housing, and the like, the world will appreciate the church in its midst, and respond to the continuing saving aspects of the Christian gospel.

What is the relation of Christ to the church? Paul magnificently sees the church as the body of Christ (I Cor. 12:27). He asserts that the Father

> has put all things under his feet and has made him the head over all things for the church, which is his body, the fulness of him who fills all in all. (Eph. 1:22-23.)

That is, the church is the full realization of him who is coming to universal fulfillment. Paul's use of the word " body " emphasizes at once the vital unity that Christians have one with another, the common Spirit that gives them life and breath, and the dependence that each member has on all the rest.

> If one member suffers, all suffer together; if one member is honored, all rejoice together. (I Cor. 12:26.)

When Christ acts in our time, he does so through his body. We are his hands to do his work. We are his feet to go on errands of mercy. We are his lips to speak the message of reconciliation. We are his mind to relate the unchanging good news to the changing circumstances of our time. Our thoughts are his thoughts. Our deeds are his deeds.

History tells us that when the church came under persecution, many were the Christians who gave themselves as martyrs to the cause. We commonly think of martyrs as those who were thrown to the wild beasts. But the word " martyr " is Greek, and does not mean one who loses his life for a cause. The word is from a verb that means " to witness." A martyr is one who bears witness to a truth. There is as much need for martyrs today as there ever was. There is a continuing call to the church and its members to be witnesses to the good news of the gospel. As a body, the church is the embodiment of Christ. The Latin word for embodiment is " incarnation." It is perhaps not too bold to claim that the church which bears witness to " the New Covenant of Our Lord and Savior Jesus Christ " is the incarnation in our time.

Index of Scripture References

Index of Names and Subjects